Rebound 1980

david r. ginglend
winifred e. stiles

Music
Activities
for retarded children

A Handbook for Teachers and Parents

ABINGDON PRESS – Nashville – New York

MUSIC ACTIVITIES FOR RETARDED CHILDREN

ISBN 0-687-27309-9

Library of Congress Catalog Card Number: 65-11516

PRINTED AND BOUND BY THE PARTHENON PRESS, AT
NASHVILLE, TENNESSEE, UNITED STATES OF AMERICA

To Mabel E. Bray, Music Educator

and

Dr. Harry N. Dubin, Educator

PREFACE

This book has been planned to assist the special music teacher, classroom teacher, recreation or volunteer leader to initiate a developmental beginning music program for retarded children or young "normal" children. The selections in this book have been arranged to aid those who may not have a background in the needs and limitations of retarded children as well as for teachers of the retarded who are looking for better ways to incorporate music into the lives of these children. We have attempted to make suggestions for the person with little or no formal training in music as well as for the trained person who may be attempting to provide a music program for these children for the first time.

The selections have been planned to appeal to children with mental ages of from three to eight years, although many of the selections cross all age levels. For example, "Stodola Pumpa" is sung by adults, teen-agers, and children everywhere. We have confined ourselves to suggesting music which, in our experience, has been successful with large numbers of retarded children in school, camp, and other kinds of recreation programs. For the most part, our presentation and approach is in terms of groups of children. This may involve many children or only a few.

In general, most of the music is suitable for "Trainable" retardates of all ages and for "Educable" retardates to about twelve years of age. Naturally there will be exceptions to all these general guides. However, from the material given there are numerous selections suitable for any group.

If you will adopt and explore this slightly different way of considering music and the retarded child, you will discover an ever expanding way of reaching and teaching the retarded child.

DAVID R. GINGLEND
WINIFRED E. STILES

ACKNOWLEDGEMENTS

We would like to thank the many parents of retarded children and the professional people who have encouraged and inspired us to pursue the theme of learning through music, especially Bernice Wells Carlson for her assistance; the National Association for Retarded Children and Newark State College for opportunities to demonstrate musical activities with groups of retarded children; Mrs. Henry Gould, Chairman, NARC Recreation Committee; Mrs. George Raymond, Director, Plainfield League for the Handicapped; Doris Hollenbach, special music teacher, Plainfield, N. J., public schools; Caryl C. Dunavan, supervisor of instructional aids, Plainfield, N. J., public schools; Gwen Ennis; Mr. and Mrs. Christopher A. Maasch; Mrs. Stanley Tobiasson; Barbara Kuscin; and the staff and campers of Happy Day Camp, Raritan Valley Unit, N.J.A.R.C.

The piano accompaniments were arranged by Miss Stiles.

CONTENTS

INTRODUCTION

Music reaches the retarded child. How often have you heard people concerned with helping retarded children make this observation? Music reaches most children. Why then is it more important for the retarded child? It is important because it is often difficult to reach him in the usual ways. His rate of development is uneven—he is capable and ready for some things before others. He may have physical or emotional problems that interfere with his rate of development. In any event, it is of the utmost importance to reach him as soon as we possibly can in order to help him identify with his environment and begin finding it a pleasant place in which to live. Failure to do so can increase his measure of frustration and add to our difficulty in helping him to grow. Music can help to accomplish this purpose and is often a first means of creating in the child a pleasurable reaction to an outside stimulus. It is often the beginning of a social relationship upon which other things may grow. Music can be one of our most effective teaching tools.

The needs of the retarded child are basically the same as those of his "normal" brother, but many factors operate to prevent his needs from being answered in exactly the same way as his brother. Most of us have witnessed how a "normal" child's need for physical activity, his need to "let off steam" and to fulfill the body's demand for growth and strength, have bypassed all artificial restrictions. Other needs, the need to express himself and to answer his growing curiosity about things in his environment, compel him to act. The needs for food, for relief of discomfort, and for attention and love are quickly transmitted with vivid communication.

The retarded child frequently, for reasons of protection, has fewer opportunities for these necessary outlets. Many of his needs have to be, or have been anticipated, and there are often problems of communication. He may have additional handicaps and may be slower to sense things and to make associations.

Every child needs a strong awareness of love and acceptance while learning to accept frustrations, restrictions, and discipline. The natural unhappiness of his parents upon discovering his retardation and in coming to terms with it are bound to have some effect upon the child. If they are unaware of his condition his inability to fulfill their natural expectations will also affect him. Likewise the attitudes of others in his immediate environment, who cannot be expected to understand his differences and limitations fully, will add to his confusion. Most important of all, he does not have the resources of the "normal" child for compensatory activities and for developing self-reliance.

The resulting problems and the magnitude that these assume frequently blind us to the fact that his needs are the same as others, that he is more alike than he is different in what he needs. The answer lies in finding slightly different ways to meet his needs rather than in trying to impose the identical pattern indicated for other children. The ways of helping him may vary according to his particular limitations and stage of development. Remember that the retarded child is an individual and must be treated with patience, love, and understanding before he can begin to develop his particular abilities.

Every child has to realize himself as a person and has to find his place in relationship to those about him. In finding this place he not only comes to know his dependency on others, but he also can come to recognize that he too has something to give. We are all dependent on others in some way. "No man is an island." We need this understanding if we are to be happy and effective in our lives. This kind of understanding begins at home and can continue at school and in other places. Music can contribute to this development. We need to begin early and to have a long-range point of view in our efforts to reach such goals.

Through the years there have been varying programs with different points of view as to the best way to educate and train retarded children. Dedicated teachers have always placed emphasis on the formation of suitable habits, habits which would be conducive to better living. By patient effort they have helped many retardates toward independent and happier lives.

Most authorities agree that failure in vocational competency among retardates is most often due to failure to get along with others, to accept criticism, to be dependable, and so on, rather than the inability to do the job involved. Teachers have recognized that being on time, completing a given task as best one can, accepting help and direction, being clean and neat, and being courteous and respectful to others are ingredients for successful living only when they are habitual. Music has much to contribute to this kind of habit development. We need to take advantage of every opportunity to consistently reinforce this kind of learning.

Goals for a Basic Music Program

Music is an area for growth. It can and should begin on a simple level and expand with the growth of the child. As in any beginning learning, a solidly familiar basic background of experiences is necessary before proceeding to more complex activities. With retarded children this background is acquired at a slower pace, and the experiences need to be repeated more often and in many different ways and settings. There is need for transitional phases in which the variations are minor and which lead slowly toward more complex responses. The variety of activities that are possible with music make this medium ideal for supplementing and reinforcing much of the desired learning for all children. In addition, music has the advantage of utilizing the "play approach" or "game technique" in learning which has always had recognized value.

Since retarded children learn more slowly and are limited in what they can learn, it is important that we present activities which will contribute to their total growth and still be within range of their abilities. We need to know why we include certain activities and to understand how they may contribute toward growth.

There seem to be at least four major areas of growth and development in which music can directly and indirectly aid all children. The music in this book has been selected to aid one, more, or all of these areas as do the "themes" under which we have grouped the selections. The music presented here has been used successfully in a variety of school and recreational programs. We have seen this music help to accomplish the following things in these four major areas:

1. Mental health. Realizing a feeling of participation, belonging, and achievement. Providing an acceptable outlet for physical and emotional tensions. Developing poise and self-confidence. Expressing feeling, and in general, fun and happiness.

2. <u>Social</u> <u>development</u> <u>and</u> <u>adjustment</u>. Group participation. Following directions. Extending attention span. Sharing and taking turns. As an aid to simple role-playing and dramatization. Appreciating social concepts. Developing self-discipline and self-control.
3. <u>Language</u> <u>development</u>. Developing auditory discrimination and memory. Learning many speech sounds and associating sounds with action, direction, and objects. Increasing vocabulary and rote learning.
4. <u>Physical</u> <u>development</u> <u>motor</u> <u>and</u> <u>muscular</u>. Using large and small muscles. Aiding co-ordination. Developing a sense of rhythm and tempo. Learning to control movement. Developing basic physical skills.

The music chosen to accomplish these goals should have a clear simple melody and strong rhythm easily felt by the children. The words should be simple, repetitious, and easily understood.

Suggestions to the Classroom Teacher, Music Teacher, or Group Leader

Music can be the one unifying activity in your program, the one activity in which every child can participate to some extent despite the degree of handicap. Music can develop group feeling and a pleasant atmosphere. A variety of short music periods throughout the day can relieve tensions and help combat restlessness due to too much sitting and concentration on more frustrating tasks. It can ease many difficult situations and contribute toward better group control.

Your attitude as leader is most important. It must be evident that you enjoy music. Never be discouraged as you work with retarded children. A severely retarded child may be absorbing and learning more than his responses reveal. Do not dwell on your fancied musical shortcomings. If you feel a bit inadequate musically, the time spent in increasing your musical ability will be most gratifying to you and your children.

The autoharp is an easy and useful accompanying instrument for those who do not play the piano. Simple instructions are found in this book. (See "How to Use the Autoharp," p. 133). While playing the autoharp you can gather the children around you, which makes for an informal, natural music period. Autoharp chords are indicated for most of the songs included in this book.

Another useful instrument is the recorder, a simple wooden flute. It is inexpensive and easy to play. A few minutes a day will lead to competency in a short time. Children love to hear the light, flute-like tone of this instrument. Most of the songs in this book may be played on the recorder or flutophone.

Many of the songs included here have been recorded—another way to present music to your children. (See "Using the Record Player," p. 132, and "Supplementary Materials," p. 137).
Remember that your enthusiasm is the most important of all teaching aids.

For the music teacher, visiting retarded children is a most rewarding experience. One cannot, of course, expect the same results as in a "normal" class, but the results may amaze you. Something happens to each child as he experiences music whether you can see a response or not.

You may find yourself doing most of the singing, and possibly most of the acting, too, until the children are sure of you and what you expect of them. They will surprise you with what they can do.

Much of the material and many of the ideas presented here are not new to you, but they have all been used successfully with classes of mildly and severely retarded children by teachers, music teachers, and group leaders. This book may serve as a guide to the kinds of songs and activities that are valuable with such classes.

As with small children, often the tempo of a song must be slowed (but not too much!) to allow the children to say the words clearly or to do the action called for. You will notice that many songs use rhythm instruments. Those children who have no speech can respond through their use. Some children are physically handicapped so that some activities are not possible for them, in which case a quieter activity is also suggested.

Consult the classroom teacher frequently as to the physical abilities of the class. She will know the warning signs of overstimulation or fatigue.

Remember always that in teaching music to retarded children the emphasis is on what music can do toward their development. The usual goals of music education must necessarily be by-passed. These children can be led to sing and play in a musical manner, however. Music can become a permanent and enjoyable part of their lives.

I
LEARNING THROUGH MUSIC

We have grouped the songs under twelve themes that are important for all children. These themes have important educational and psychological considerations in planning a program or curriculum for the retarded child, and we have given a few indications of what makes them particularly important for him. Take the time to think about these themes and you will realize that these are areas of interest to children and provide a framework for many activities in which you can help the child to grow and learn.

We do not suggest that these themes are comprehensive. Obviously, they could be subdivided into numerous other themes or condensed into a few. They are interrelated, hence many songs will fit under more than one theme.

As you become familiar with the songs, you will find many ways to change words, add new verses, vary actions, and increase the kinds of responses you want from your particular group in terms of increasing skill and meeting the needs of growth.

1. All About Me

Self-realization is an all important principle in mental health. An awareness of self can begin with the recognition that I have eyes, ears, a nose, et cetera. Children all go through a "me" stage, with a whole catagory of things "I" know, like, and can do.

In addition to self-realization, the child needs to know his place in the family. The achievement of simple courtesy and manners will make every child's life more pleasant and will increase his opportunities for family and social acceptance. Caring for his personal needs will improve his appearance and make him less dependent on others.

The retarded child also needs to know basic things about the community in which he lives. Usually his experience has been limited. Songs, rhymes, stories, and trips can add to this understanding.

It is of utmost importance that he be helped to form habits of safety and health at home, at school, on the playground, and in the community. All of this knowledge can add to his sense of security and well-being.

2. Listen!

Listening requires continuous development in all children. A child needs to listen in order to know what people have said or asked, to know what we are going to do and when we are going to do it. He also needs to know what to listen for. He cannot react to music unless he listens consciously and with awareness.

Auditory discrimination is vital and basic in the development of communication and language. Listening will aid in his understanding of many abstract words, such as loud and soft, fast and slow, up and down.

This important sense training will help a child to follow directions, to begin to focus his attention and to listen to many things other than music. He will be aided by something to watch as well. This something can be you—the teacher or leader.

3. Ten Little Fingers

Children have always responded to and liked finger plays. They involve imagination, imitation, and watching. At first the children will concentrate on doing the actions as you sing. Do not expect them to do two things at once. Eventually, however, some children will learn the words and sing along.

Obviously these finger plays are exercises for the weak small muscles of the hands and fingers. A finger play is an excellent device for gaining the attention of a group as well as a relaxing activity that may precede the introduction of a new activity.

4. I Can! Can You?

All children like to show what they know and can do and need opportunities to do so. There is a challenge present in these songs. Retarded children need the opportunity to learn to choose and to make decisions in a simple way—such as, what song shall we sing? What game shall we play next? Guessing delights all children, and being able to "not tell" when one knows the answer is basic to learning self-control. Following directions and abiding by the rules of an activity are important learnings for retarded children. When guessing what instrument was played the child must remember that it is important to confine answers to instruments and not to other categories of things that may be involved in another guessing game.

5. Holidays Are Happy Days

Holidays are special days, and children look forward to them with great anticipation. Retarded children are no exception. These days give them some sense of time and help to form a frame of reference for the seasons of the year.

Most months contain some holiday, and these are sometimes helpful in aiding a child in learning the months of the year. This is a fairly abstract idea for most retarded children, however, and not nearly as meaningful as knowing that fall brings Halloween and Thanksgiving, winter brings Christmas and Valentine's Day, and so on.

Holidays help to give a sense of routine and stability. They are times to talk about, to sing about, to make things for, to dramatize, and to celebrate. Most important, holidays are times to look forward to and to recall. Don't forget that a child's birthday is as important as any of them!

6. Things to Learn

The concept of learning is as important to children as it is to the teacher or leader. Although the retarded child is limited in what he can learn, it is vital to keep the idea of learning and work a large part of every day. Remember that achievement is necessary for everyone. Small learnings, such as counting to ten or knowing what comes next in a song or game, are major achievements for retarded children and should be recognized and praised as such.

It is important to help retarded children to distinguish between play and fun and those activities which require listening and practice for learning. Learning and work should be pleasant. Music can help in these areas. The important thing to strive for is a balanced program. Listening, self-control, cooperation, and increased ability to do things alone and with others are the necessary things to learn.

7. Let's Make Music

All children can make music and delight in doing so. This whole book is about just that. Performing in a group with rhythm instruments is an enjoyable activity for retarded children. Having learned how to hold and play the instruments separately, the children can make group activity a real contribution toward listening, establishing a sense of rhythm, and developing self-control—when to play and when not to play.

8. Now Let's Play

Magic words indeed for all children! Try to develop a period of free and imaginative play as well as the more organized forms of play. Frequent shorter periods of play spaced throughout the day are more beneficial to the retarded child than one concentrated period. There are many kinds of play—active and quiet, group and solitary—and a variety of games serving different needs and purposes. Remember that children grow and learn through play. It is one of their basic needs. There is always time in the day to fit in a parade, a game of squat tag, or a finger play between other activities.

9. Quiet Time

Many young children become overstimulated and sometimes disorganized from prolonged activity. Bodies and spirits need the restorative quality of a quiet time. It may be a rest period or a time when the children listen quietly for sounds outside the room. It may be listening quietly to soothing music or to a familiar story. Maria Montessori detailed the great need for the "silenzio" in a child's day.

Every child needs simple quiet songs like those given here. He sings them in a group and is calmed, but he also often sings them to himself. They are frequently a source of solace and comfort to him or an expression of quiet well-being. The range of such songs is quite wide, and the music is generally more important than the words in establishing the mood. We have known many retarded children to hum or sing a number of these songs during play or while working quietly at some table task.

The retarded child can profit greatly from the awareness of God's love and protection. It can be for him, as it is for many of us, a source of comfort and security in times of stress and worry. Simple prayers can give meaning to the day's routine and be the beginning of an inner control for retarded children. Suitable nonsectarian prayers and spirituals have a quieting effect that is beneficial to all children.

10. Let's Pretend

The magic world of make-believe is universal. Retarded children need help and encouragement in the initial stages of pretending. Given this help, they will amaze you with how they reflect the world they know, the attitudes of others, and their own feelings about things. Pretending and dramatization, begun simply in songs, can lead to the dramatization of simple stories. It can help the child to express himself as well. Almost every song provides the children some opportunity to be someone or something other than himself. The ability to carry through a complete story is an important achievement for young children.

11. Just for Fun

To many retarded children anything that they can do well is fun, but everyone needs to "bubble over," to laugh and be silly, and to enjoy a bit of nonsense from time to time. There are important learnings involved in distinguishing between what is nonsense and fun and what is not. A sense of humor is as important for everyone as is the need to have fun. When you finally hear the laughter of a child who has been withdrawn, overanxious, or tense, you will need no further convincing of the therapy of laughter.

12. Come to the Party

All children love parties. They are fun to look forward to, and they provide happy memories. Retarded children need many experiences with parties before they become a natural part of the children's school and home background.

The theme of a party may vary, but the routine of activities should remain the same. Simple refreshments and favors are best, with the activities drawn from familiar games and dances.

As the children grow in ability to participate in parties, they will delight in planning with the teacher or leader. Each child may choose a game or dance sometime before the party. An announcement that this is Mary's game or Bobby's dance makes each child feel that he is an important part of the party and contributes indirectly toward other social learnings.

II
SONG MATERIAL

Here is the music. You will note that the suggested activities listed for each song are in order of difficulty of performance, with the simplest listed first, a more difficult one next, and so on. Repeat each activity in only one way until all the children are familiar with it before trying the variations.

General Suggestions

The retarded child will not become bored by frequent repetition of these musical activities. In fact, as they become familiar to him, you will see him relax and enjoy them. Each variation becomes an almost new activity. The retarded child needs this gradual progression from the known to the unknown and, when given a chance to choose will invariably select the most familiar activity, the one in which he feels most comfortable and in which he knows what is expected of him.

Help the child to <u>listen</u> to the music. He cannot respond rhythmically to music unless he consciously listens to it. This requires continuous development in all children.

Never try to do anything with rhythm instruments to a song that is being sung until the children know it well. Trying to do two things at once—singing and playing—is too difficult.

Many young retarded children tire easily and have short attention spans. Frequent activities of short duration can grow into more extended ones. Comparatively quiet activities should be alternated with more strenuous ones.

You will have to determine your children's abilities, but when in doubt, begin on the simplest level. Temper new songs with the known and familiar ones and keep the accent on enjoyment and fun!

Amaryllis

HENRI GHYS

As a rhythm band activity:

1. Beat the melody rhythm with the sticks all the way through.

2. Using the triangle play 1, 2, 3, 4, all the way through.

3. On the tambourine tap 1, 2, 3, rest, all the way through.

4. When the children are familiar with the melody and their own parts, combine the instruments. Try to keep each instrument beating its own rhythm.

Angels Watching Over Me

Angel Band

Traditional Melody

There was one, there were two, there were three lit-tle an-gels, There were four, there were five, there were six, lit-tle an-gels, There were sev-en, there were eight, there were nine, lit-tle an-gels, Ten lit-tle an-gels in the band. Oh, was-n't that a band, Sun-day morn-ing, Sun-day morn-ing, Sun-day

morn-ing, Was-n't that a band, Sun - day morn-ing, Sun - day morn-ing soon.

1. Use fingers to count the angels.
Clap during the chorus.

2. Substitute instruments for angels.

> There was one, there were two, there were three little trumpets.
> Chorus: "Toot, toot, toot, toot, et cetera."

> Drums—rat-tat-tat.   Trombones—loo, loo, loo.   Flutes—whistle.

The Band

Traditional

This is the way we play the drum, play the drum, play the drum.

This is the way we play the drum When we play in the band.

Add other rhythm instruments or standard instruments. Play the rhythm instruments and pantomime the others.

> Last verse: This is the way we play them all
> When we play in the band.

Before We Play

D.R.G. - B.W.C.

W.E.S.

1. Act out song:

A, A, what shall we play? .... *Hands folded.*
E, E, what will it be? .... *Open palms in questioning gesture.*
I, I, point to the sky, ... *Point upward.*
O, O, the ground is below .... *Point to ground.*
U, U, what shall we do? .... *Point to each other.*
Now our letters are through.
A, E, I, O, and U.
Now let's try something new.

2. A child may play a triangle, finger cymbals, or bells on the vowel sounds. Some children may be able to play the vowel tones on resonater bells or the piano. Using a crayon, draw the letter on the piano key.

3. The children may sing the vowels while the teacher sings the rest of the song.

4. One child may sing the vowels as the rest of the group sings the following words.

Come with Me

Italian Folk Song

Come walk-ing with me, Come walk-ing with me, O-ver the high-way and down to the sea, Come walk-ing with me.

Come dancing me.

Come tiptoe with me.

Come singing with me.

Come skating with me.

1. In addition to singing the words of this lovely melody, hum it, sing it with vowel sounds—ah, oh, oo, et cetera—or any pleasing combination, such as la, lo, et cetera.

2. All the children interpret the action independently.

3. One child may be selected to stand before his chosen partner and sing, "Come walking with me." They then go hand in hand around the room as the rest of the group sings.

4. One child may sing to another, "George, come follow me." George follows. At the end of the verse, the first child sits down and George sings to another child using his name in the song.

5. One child may sing to a chosen partner using his name as above. The group will sing the action desired as the two children walk, skate, dance, et cetera.

Birthday Song

W.E.S.

"My Dreydl" by S. GOLDFARB

To - day is some - one's birth - day; That some-one is right here, We'll wish him "Hap - py Birth - day!" and a ver - y hap - py year. Oh, (her)

Hap - py, hap - py birth - day, and a ver - y hap - py year! Oh,

Hap - py, hap - py birth - day, and a ver - y hap - py year!

Use the names of the children in your group. For example:

> 2. Today is Barbara's birthday and Barbara is right here!
> We'll wish her happy birthday and a very happy year.
> Oh, happy birthday, Barbara, and a very happy year,
> Oh, happy birthday, Barbara, and a very happy year!

Chiapanecas

D.R.G.

Mexican Dance Song

Come, all you chil - dren, clap hands (clap, clap) Come, all you

chil - dren, clap hands, (clap, clap) Come, all you chil - dren, clap

FINE

hands (clap, clap) Come all you chil - dren, clap hands (clap, clap)

La, la, la, la, la, la, la, etc.

This song has two melodies—"A" and "B" with a return to the "A" melody.

1. Sing the words, clapping at the end of each phrase as indicated. While singing "La, la" thrust each arm alternately as if playing maracas.

2. When these words and the activities are familiar, additional fun and listening experience are gained by substituting:

> Come, everybody, stamp feet!
> Now just the boys clap hands!
> Now just the girls clap hands! et cetera

3. Using sticks and other instruments, sing, "Now all you children play sticks", et cetera. Use maracas or tambourines on the "B" part.

4. Choose three different instruments. Each one will play after one phrase, all play after the fourth phrase. During the "B" section the drum or tambourine could play "1" in each measure and the sticks play "1, 2, 3."

Chopsticks

Traditional Melody

FINE

D.C.

This piece has two different melodies—"A" and "B."

1. Counting "*1, 2, 3,*" play section "A" with rhythm sticks. Listen to section "B" and play again when "A" returns.

2. A drum may play "*1*" on each measure as the sticks continue to play "*1, 2, 3.*" On section "B" the tambourine or triangle plays "*3, 1*" through the entire section. Listen to the melody to get started.
When section "A" returns, the drum and sticks play as before.

3. Using the first part of No. 2 above, select a different instrument to play with the drum on the last section "A" instead of sticks.

Come and Ride Our Train

Brazilian Folk Song

Choo, choo, choo, choo, choo, choo, choo, choo, Come and ride our train.

Choo, choo, choo, choo, choo, choo, choo, choo, Rid-ing on our train.

Choo, choo, choo, choo, choo, choo, choo, choo, Come and take a ride.

Choo, choo, choo, choo, choo, choo, choo, choo, Tra-vel far and wide.

Whoooo - - - - - - - - - - - Whoooo - - - - - - - - - - Whoooo!

1. Sand blocks make a grand accompaniment for this song. Be sure to pull the cord for the whistle!

2. Show the children how to slide their feet in short steps without lifting them from the floor. Ask the children what their feet are "saying."

3. Individual children may be the train while the group sings. They must listen carefully as the train goes faster or slower.

4. Form a train with the smallest and slowest children in front and larger and more able children at the rear. Start slowly and keep in time. Gradually go faster, then slow down and come to a stop.

The Cuckoo Clock

Traditional Melody

38

1. First section: Clap hands from side to side.

On holds preceding chorus: Slap hands on knees rapidly.

Chorus (3 beats to each measure): 1. Slap knees 2. Clap hands 3. Snap fingers. Practice this part very slowly without the music several times.

Add one more "Cuckoo" on each succeeding verse, remembering to add a snap as well. Add the notes needed in the piano part. This will, of course, add beats to the "Cuckoo" measures.

2. Vary the first section by snapping fingers, holding the hands together and moving them back and forth, et cetera.

3. Using rhythm sticks "clap" them from side to side on the first part, tap quickly on the floor during the holds, tap rhythm of the melody in the chorus, emphasizing the "Cuckoo."

4. Use a woodblock during the first section, trill a triangle on the holds, use sticks for the chorus.

God Is Love

Traditional

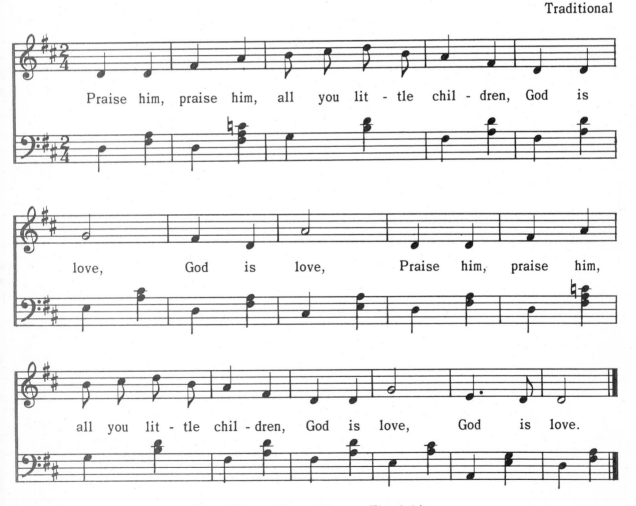

Love him.   Serve him.   Thank him.

Days of the Week

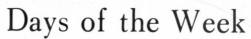

W.E.S.

W.E.S.

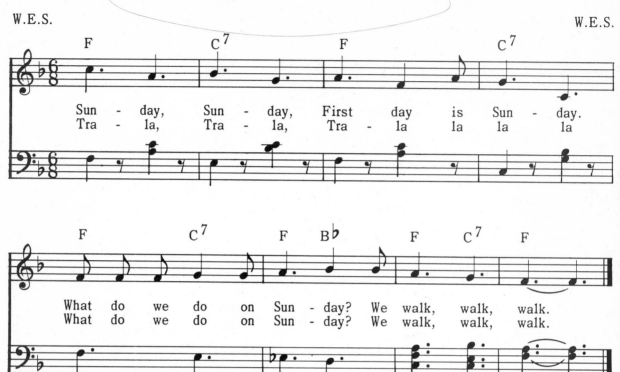

Sun - day, Sun - day, First day is Sun - day.
Tra - la, Tra - la, Tra - la la la la

What do we do on Sun - day? We walk, walk, walk.
What do we do on Sun - day? We walk, walk, walk.

2. Monday, Monday, Second day is Monday,
   What do we do on Monday? We skip, skip, skip.

3. Tuesday—slide.

4. Wednesday—run.

5. Thursday—tip, tip, toe.

6. Friday—jump.

7. Saturday—hop.

1. The entire group may do this together. Stand still on the first part when the question is asked. Perform the action when the "Trala's" start.

2. Seven children may be selected to be the days of the week. They stand in front of the group and must remember the day of the week they represent and perform the action for their day at the proper time.

Did You Ever?

Adapted

Alabama Folk Song

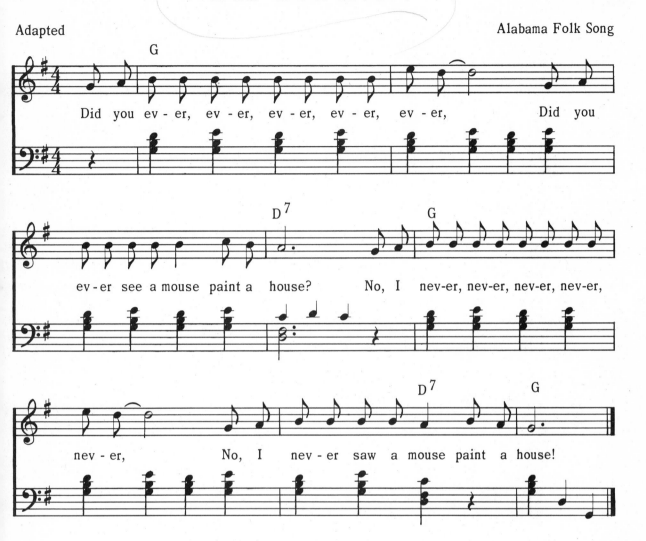

Did you ever, ev-er, ev-er, ev-er, ev-er, Did you ev-er see a mouse paint a house? No, I nev-er, nev-er, nev-er, nev-er, nev-er, No, I nev-er saw a mouse paint a house!

Did you ever see a pig dance a jig?

Did you ever see a crow shovel snow?

Did you ever see a snake bake a cake?

Did you ever see a fish wash a dish?

Did you ever see a goat sail a boat?

Did you ever see a snail wave his tail?

Did you ever see a cat wear a hat?

Did you ever see a sheep drive a jeep?

Dinah

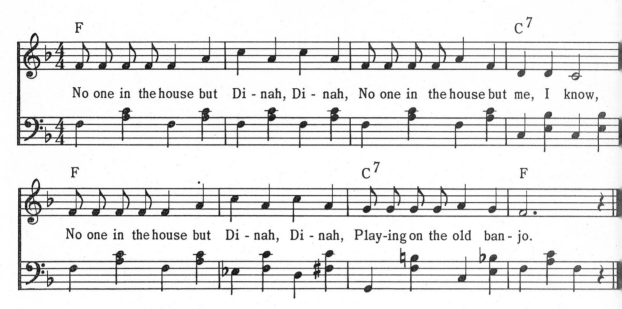

No one in the house but Di - nah, Di - nah, No one in the house but me, I know,

No one in the house but Di - nah, Di - nah, Play-ing on the old ban - jo.

Adapted by permission of American Book Company from *The American Singer,* 2nd ed., Book III, by John W. Beattie, Josephine Wolverton, Grace V. Wilson, and Howard Hinga.

Plink, plinka-plink, plink, plink, plink, plink, plink, et cetera.

No one in the house but Dinah, Dinah, no one in the house when I came in,
No one in the house but Dinah, Dinah, Playing on the violin.
La, la, la, la, et cetera.

No one in the house but me alone . . . Playing on the big trombone.
Too, too, too, too, et cetera.

No one in the house but me, I say . . . Playing on the cymbals gay.
Zing, zing, zing, et cetera.

No one in the house whenever I come . . . Playing on the big bass drum.
Boom, booma, boom, et cetera.

1. Sing the verses, then dramatize and sing the sound the instrument makes.
2. In a larger group, different rows of children play the same instrument each time as more instruments are sung about. They must remember their instrument.

Here is another version of this favorite song:

Someone's in the house with Dinah, Dinah,
Someone's in the house—it's Mrs. Dix,
Someone's in the house with Dinah, Dinah,
Playing on the rhythm sticks.

It's Mrs. Wells . . Playing on the jingle bells. It's Mrs. Blum . . Playing on the little drum.

It's Mrs. Green . . Playing on the tambourine. The music's grand . . Playing in the rhythm band

3. Select a child or children for the various instruments. Wait for the right verse to play
Everyone plays on the last verse.

Do, Lord

Traditional Melody

Do, Lord, Oh, do, Lord, Oh, do re-mem-ber me. Do, Lord, Oh, do, Lord, Oh, do re-mem-ber me. Do, Lord, oh, do, Lord, Oh, do re-mem-ber me, Way be-yond the blue.

I've got a home in glory land that outshines the sun.

Now, I'm going up to glory, open the gates.

God loves all his many children, and he loves me too.

Be kind to ev'ryone you meet and they'll be kind to you.

The Lord loves ev'ryone of us, and we all love him too.

The Lord is always by our side, oh he knows what we do.

Improvise other verses or choose favorite verses learned from time to time.

Down in the Valley

Traditional Melody

Sing me a song, dear, sing, "I love you,"
  Sing me a song, dear, I'll sing it too.
I'll sing it, too, dear, I'll sing it too,
  Sing me a song, dear, I'll sing it too.

Writing this letter containing three lines
  Answer my question, "Will you be mine?"
"Will you be mine, dear? Will you be mine?"
  Answer my question, "Will you be mine?"

Build me a castle up in the sky,
  Build me a castle with clouds floating by.
Clouds floating by, dear, clouds floating by,
  Build me a castle with clouds floating by.

Roses love sunshine, violets love dew,
  Angels in heaven know I love you.
Know I love you, dear, know I love you,
  Angels in heaven know I love you.

This is another melody to hum or sing with neutral syllables.

Jack in the Box

Traditional

W.E.S.

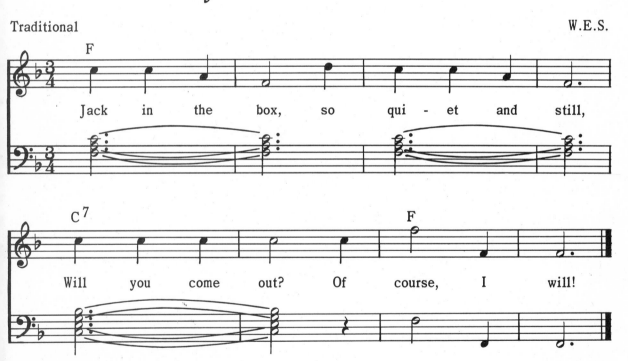

1. Children have thumbs against the palm of the hand with the fingers hiding the thumb. At the end of the song they let their thumbs pop out.

2. As a large muscle activity, the children are crouched in a squatting position. At the end of the song they jump up to a standing position, jumping up and down like a Jack released from his box.

Elephant Song

Chilean Folk Song

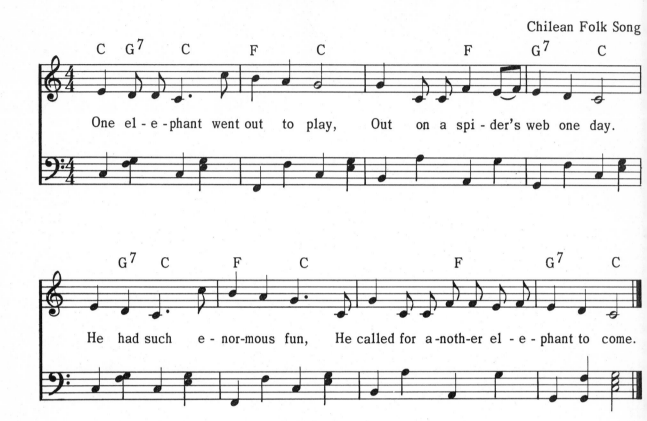

One el-e-phant went out to play, Out on a spi-der's web one day.

He had such e-nor-mous fun, He called for a-noth-er el-e-phant to come.

Two elephants went out to play
Out on a spider's web one day,
They had such enormous fun,
They called for another elephant to come.

1. Select one child to be the elephant. He chooses the second elephant, et cetera. Continue until "They called for another but there were none." If there is not time for each child, call for "All the elephants to come."

2. This activity involves the back and shoulder muscles which are not exercised enough. The child bends over with hands clasped to make a trunk. Remember that the trunk is an extension of your nose. Bend way over—low enough to pick peanuts off the floor! The child sways his trunk and walks heavily in time with the music. He chooses another elephant to join him at the end of the verse. That elephant chooses yet another and so on.

3. Using instruments and sitting in a circle, the first elephant plays his instrument during the first verse. The elephant he chooses joins him in the next verse. Each verse adds an instrument until all are playing.

Listen!

W.E.S.   W.E.S.

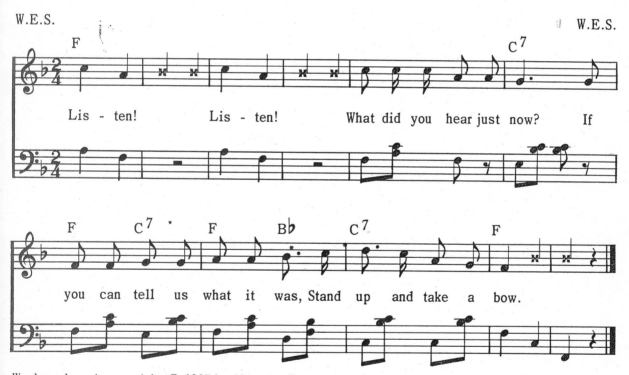

Lis - ten!   Lis - ten!   What did you   hear just now?   If

you can tell   us what it was, Stand up   and take   a   bow.

1. Place several rhythm instruments where children cannot see them. Play one of them in the places marked in the song. All children take a bow. Choose one child and ask, "Do you know what the instrument was?" If he guesses correctly, he may play the next instrument. Be sure to wait for the right time to play.

2. Instead of playing instruments, the teacher may whisper a word softly in the place marked.

Ev'rybody

Traditional Melody

Ev - 'ry - bod - y likes to go to school,

Ev - 'ry - bod - y likes to go to school,

Ev - 'ry - bod - y, ev - 'ry - bod - y, ev - 'ry - bod - y, ev - 'ry - bod - y

Ev - 'ry - bod - y likes to go to school.

1. Add verses about the school day, such as: Everybody likes to do his work, take a nap, run and play.

Or motions: Everybody likes to slide his feet, clap his hands, tap his toes.

Activities at home: Everybody likes to brush his teeth, comb his hair, shine his shoes, wash his hands.

Playing in rhythm band: Everybody likes to play in the band, play the drum, click the sticks, ring a bell, shake, shake, shake (for tambourine).

Pantomime the actions. Children will suggest many more things that everybody likes to do.

2. Play with rhythm sticks.

3. Play on the bongo drums.

4. Choose different instruments or combinations of instruments to play on various verses.

Greeting Song

French Folk Song

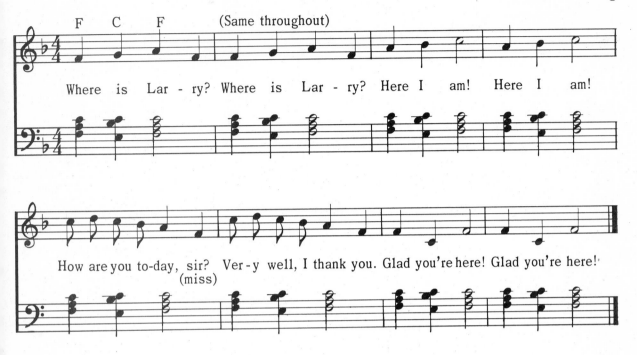

Where is Lar - ry? Where is Lar - ry? Here I am! Here I am!

How are you to-day, sir? Ver-y well, I thank you. Glad you're here! Glad you're here!
(miss)

1. Call roll using names of children in your group:

Where is Larry?	*Leader sings.*
Here I am!	*Child answers.*
How are you today, sir?	*Leader sings.*
Very well, I thank you.	*Child answers.*
Glad you're here!	*All children sing.*

If there are some children with no speech, they may answer by playing rhythm instruments on "Here I am!" (1, 2, 3) and "Very well, I thank you!" (1-2, 3-4,5, 6). All the children will want to play the instruments. Those with speech will sing as well as play.

2. Use this melody with the traditional words, "Frere Jacques," and "Where Is Thumbkin," the finger play.

3. Many other verses can be devised. During the day, "Are you working?" "Time for resting, time for resting, everyone, everyone," "Let's get ready," et cetera, may produce faster results than a spoken question or direction.

Five Little Pumpkins

Unknown

L. B. P.

1. This song may be done as a finger play, touching or bending down the finger being sung about, and doing such action as may be indicated.

2. Five children may be selected to be the pumpkins, each singing his own line, (with your help if necessary). One child may be the wind.

3. Choose five different instruments to be the voices of the pumpkins. Be sure to make each instrument "say" the words.

4. This song lends itself to many occasions. You will doubtless think of others besides the versions below.

5. Pictures, finger puppets, stick puppets, and the flannelboard will all add to the enjoyment of this song.

Additional Verses

Five Little Snowflakes

Five little snowflakes sitting on a gate,
 The first one said, "Oh my, it's getting late!"
The second one said, "Jack Frost is in the air."
 The third one said, "But we don't care!"
The fourth one said, "Let's whirl and whirl away"
 The fifth one said, "It's such a sunny day."
"Oooooo," went the wind and out went the sun,
 And the five little snowflakes had a lot of fun.

Five Little Campers

Five little campers sitting in the sun,
 The first one said, "I'd like to have some fun."
The second one said, "Let's all go for a swim,"
 The third one said, "I'll be the first one in!"
The fourth one said, "Let's dive into the pool,"
 The fifth one said, "Oh, my, the water's cool!"
"Oooooo," went the wind and in went the sun,
 And the five little campers all began to run.

Five Little Cowboys

Five little cowboys sitting on a gate,
 The first one said, "Gee, rodeos are great!"
The second one said, "There are buzzards in the air."
 The third one said, "But we don't care."
The fourth one said, "Let's watch the horses run."
 The fifth one said, "I'm ready for some fun."
"Oooooo," went the wind and off went their hats,
 And the five little cowboys fell from where they sat.

Five Little Spacemen

Five little spacemen sitting on the stars,
 The first one said, "Let's all fly up to Mars."
The second one said, "There are rockets in the air."
 The third one said, "But we don't care."
The fourth one said, "Let's fly away so high,"
 The fifth one said, "Let's go up in the sky."
Then swish went the ship and out went the light,
 And the five little spacemen flew right out of sight.

51

Good-bye, My Darling

Traditional Melody

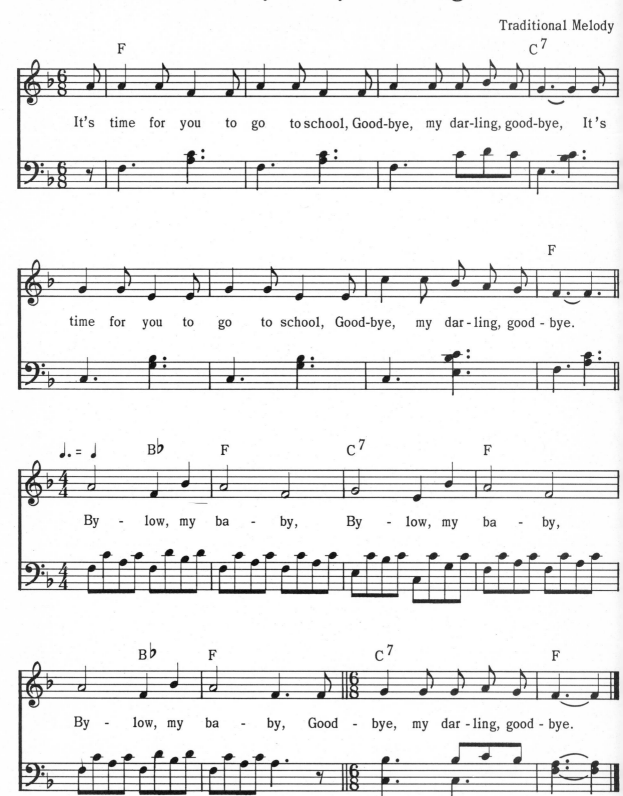

It's time for you to go to school, Good-bye, my dar-ling, good-bye, It's

time for you to go to school, Good-bye, my dar-ling, good-bye.

By - low, my ba - by, By - low, my ba - by,

By - low, my ba - by, Good - bye, my dar - ling, good - bye.

Hurry before you miss the bus.

Don't forget to take your lunch.

I'll be here when you come home.

1. Make up other verses suitable for your group. In the version above we sing as our mothers might sing to us when we are getting ready for school or day camp.
As a closing song these verses might be used:

It's almost time to close the camp (school).

Don't forget to say your prayers.

Don't forget your friends at camp (school).

Larry and Billy, go get your coats.

Don't forget to brush your teeth.

2. During the chorus, children may rock gently from side to side or pretend to rock a baby. Sometimes hum or sing a neutral syllable during the chorus.

Thank You, God

Unknown

W.E.S.

Thank you for the world so sweet, Thank you for the food we eat,

Thank you for the birds that sing, Thank you, God, for ev - 'ry - thing.

Good Manners

JAMES PIERPONT
Adapted

W.E.S.-D.R.G.

I know what to do When I'm in-tro-duced to you. I

smile and shake your hand And say, "How do you do?"

CHORUS

"How do you do?" and "Par-don me," will help you on your way;

"Please" and "Thank you" will make a pleas-ant day;

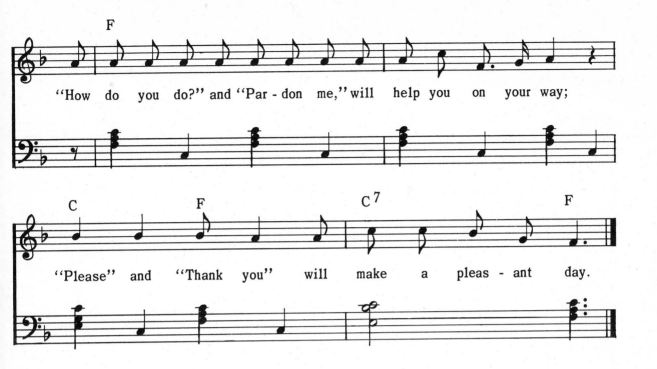

"How do you do?" and "Par - don me," will help you on your way;

"Please" and "Thank you" will make a pleas - ant day.

I like to talk to you,
  But I can listen, too.
Say, "Pardon me, what did you say?"
  When I do not hear you.
Chorus.

Now here's a word to say
  At home, or school, or play—
It's "Please, may I have this or that."
  I use it every day.
Chorus

When presents come my way
  Or you help me through the day,
Then "Thank you," with a merry smile,
  Is what I always say.
Chorus.

Ha, Ha, This-a-way

American Folk Song

This song can be very active, or it can be a "sit in place" activity.

1. When you use it as an active song, the children stand in place during the chorus and do the action indicated in the verse.

Ha, ha, this-away,	*Clap hands on "Ha, ha"; put one hand and arm out to side on "this-away."*
Ha, ha, that-away,	*Clap as above, put other hand out.*
Ha, ha, this-away,	*Clap as above, hand out.*
All day long.	*Clap twice, slap thighs on "long."*

Now we go jumping, hopping, skipping, sliding, tiptoe, walking, twirling, flying, et cetera. Then we jump, hop, skip, slide, back again.

2. Sitting in place:
Now we do some clapping, tapping, rocking, nodding, snapping, shaking, bouncing, et cetera.
Everyone is clapping, tapping, rocking, et cetera.

3. Using instruments:
Listen to us clicking, tapping, shaking, ringing, drumming, et cetera.

4. Another version:

When I was a little girl (or boy)
I used to play at jump the rope, bounce the ball, patty-cake, et cetera.
I had a little mama doll, kiddie car, bouncing ball, et cetera.

Halloween Is Coming

D.R.G. - W.E.S.

Traditional Melody

Hal - lo - ween is com - ing, Ha, ha, ha! Hal - lo - ween is com - ing, Hee, hee, hee!

Spooks will prowl on Hal - lo - ween,

Bats and gob - lins will soon be seen, Ghosts will float right

through the air, Witch - es on broom-sticks will give you a scare.

Halloween is coming, Ha, ha, ha!
Halloween is coming, Hee, hee, hee!
Jack-o'-lanterns burning bright
Will look out of windows on Halloween night.
Ghosts and witches, goblins, too,
On Halloween are out to scare you. Boo!

Helping

W.E.S. W.E.S.

I help my moth-er ev-'ry day, ev-'ry day, ev-'ry day, I

help my moth-er ev-'ry day, Ev-'ry day I can.

Children add verses such as:

> I pick my clothes up every day.
>
> I wipe the dishes everyday.
>
> I set the table everyday.
>
> I always wear a happy smile.

Vary this with: "I help my teacher," and "I help my father," followed in each case by ways to help teacher or father.

Here Is the Church

Traditional

W.E.S.

Finger play:

Here is the church,	*Fingers interlocked.*
Here is the steeple,	*Index fingers up.*
Open the door	*Turn hands over.*
And see all the people.	*Wiggle fingers.*
First they sing,	*Hold hymn book.*
And then they pray	*Fold hands.*
And then they quietly walk away.	*Fingers "walk" away.*

If children have trouble with the first hand position, holding the hands knuckle to knuckle works just as well.

* Autoharp accomp. in key of C.

He's Got the Whole World

American Spiritual

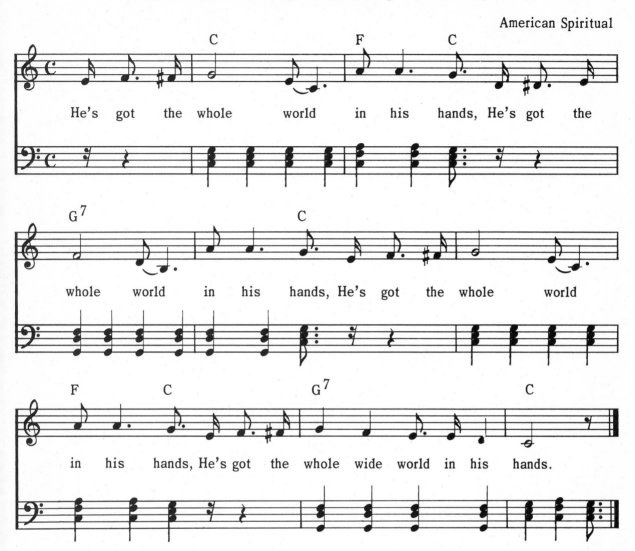

He's got the whole world in his hands, He's got the whole world in his hands, He's got the whole world in his hands, He's got the whole wide world in his hands.

Add verses suggested by the children, such as:

the names of those present — two at a time

You and me	The sun and the moon
Mommy and Daddy	The wind and the rain
Little bitty baby	The fish in the sea
Brother and sister	The birds of the air
All of us here	Name of the school or camp

If You're Happy

Traditional Melody

1. Suggest actions that may be done sitting down such as tap your head, tap your feet, shake your hands, wink your eye, wave good-bye. Wait for the right time to make the motions.

2. Add actions that dramatize daily happenings—wash your hands, shine your shoes, comb your hair, say your prayers, dust the chair, iron your clothes, et cetera.

3. For an active game children stand in a circle and perform the action you suggest—touch your toes, take a bow, turn around, jump up high, step so high, touch the sky, that's enough, et cetera.

I Take My Little Hands

As sung by B. KUSCIN

1. Dramatize: "I take my little hands and go clap, clap, clap." Add other actions such as feet, stamp; fingers, snap; toes, tap; eyes, wink; head, shake; finger, point.

2. Using rhythm instruments, sing "I take my little sticks and go click-click-click." Only the children with sticks will play for that verse. Continue using other instruments.

I Have a Little Rooster

Traditional Melody

I have a little roos-ter by the barn - yard gate, And
I have a little hen by the barn - yard gate, And

that lit - tle roos-ter is my play-mate, *omit in first verse; repeat as
that lit - tle hen is my play-mate, And that lit - tle hen goes

necessary in later verses.
"Cluck, cluck, cluck, And that lit - tle roos - ter goes,

"Cock - a - doo - dle - doo! Doo, doo, doo, doo, doo, dood - ley, doo!"

Rooster—cock-a-doodle-doo. *Cup hands around mouth.*

Hen—cluck, cluck, cluck. *With thumb and fingers of one hand together, make a pecking motion in palm of other hand.*

Duck—quack, quack, quack. *With palms together, open and shut them.*

Pig—oink, oink, oink. *Press palms of hands against the cheeks.*

Donkey—Hee, hee, haw. *Place thumbs just above the ears on either side of the head and wiggle the fingers.*

Turkey—gobble, gobble, gobble.	*Grasp the flesh under the chin with the* *thumb and first finger.*
Pony—trot, trot, trot.	*Slap knees or stamp feet.*
Kitten—purr, purr, purr.	*Pretend to stroke the cat.*
Bird—tweet, tweet, tweet.	*Interlock thumbs and flap hands.*

Begin teaching this song by using only three or four verses until the children are completely familiar with them. Gradually add a new verse from time to time always keeping the same order. The motion accompanying the animal sound serves too as an extra memory cue as well as adding fun and providing action for small muscles.

After each new verse the group sings back through the sounds, repeating the measure indicated as many times as necessary, always ending with the rooster's "doodley doo." For example:

And that little duck goes, "Quack, quack, quack,"
And that little hen goes, "Cluck, cluck, cluck,"
And that little rooster goes, et cetera.

Mary Had a Baby

American Spiritual

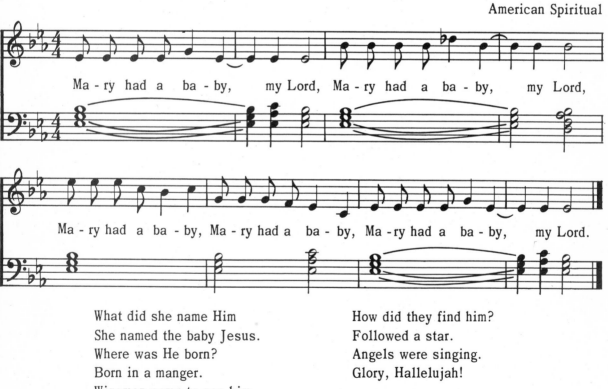

What did she name Him
She named the baby Jesus.
Where was He born?
Born in a manger.
Wisemen came to see him.

How did they find him?
Followed a star.
Angels were singing.
Glory, Hallelujah!

This lovely spiritual lends itself to simple dramatization of the Christmas story.

Use the flannel board to tell the story. The children could add the various cutouts at the right time.

Indians

W.E.S.

W.E.S.

See the In - dian chief Beat up - on his drum,

Hi - ya, hi - ya, Hi - ya, hi - ya, Hi - ya, hi - ya, Ho!

See the Indian braves walking Indian file.

See the Indian squaws grinding yellow corn.

See the Indian boys paddling their canoes.

See the Indian girls making bowls of clay.

See the Indian braves dance around the fire.

1. Dramatize the verses of the song. Slap knees on "Hiya" accenting the beginning of each measure. Raise hands high after slapping knees on "Ho!"
2. Beat a tom-tom on the chorus.
3. Use shakers on the chorus.
4. Use shakers during the verses, tom-tom on the chorus.
5. Standing in a circle take 4 steps toward center on measures 1, 2,
   4 steps back on measures 3, 4
   6 toe-heel steps around in a circle on 5, 6, 7
   Stamp on "Ho!" on measure 8.

Skipping Is Fun

Traditional Melody, adapted

Skip-ping is fun, oh, skip-ping is fun! Skip-ping is fun for ev-'ry-one! The more you skip, the bet-ter you skip, So keep on skip-ping, Skip-pi-ty, skip!

Words from *Songs and Marching Tunes for Children* by Paul Edmonds.
Used by permission of Sir Isaac Pitman and Sons, Ltd.

1. Let the children suggest things to do that are fun. <u>You</u> may not think that some of them are fun but that is not important.

Jumping	Marching	Singing	Swinging	Dusting	Sweeping
Running	Dancing	Sliding	Swimming	Washing	Cooking
Walking	Hopping	Skating	Rocking	Ironing	Painting

2. Let the children look for pictures of things that are fun. Mount them on construction paper, and make selections from the picture when you sing this song.

It's Easter

W.E.S.

G. F. ROOT

Bells are ring - ing, bells are ring - ing for East - er, for East - er, Chil - dren sing - ing, chil - dren sing - ing for glad East - er - time. Al - le - lu - ia! Al - le - lu - ia! It's East - er, It's East - er! Al - le - lu - ia! Al - le - lu - ia! It's glad East - er - time.

2. Flowers growing,
   Breezes blowing.

3. Carols singing,
   Praises bringing.

Little Fish

D.R.G. - B.W.C.

W.E.S.

Lit - tle fish goes out to play, He wig - gles his fins, then swims a - way; He swims and swims in the wa - ter bright, He o - pens his mouth and takes a bite! Mmmmmmmmm! Tastes good!

This may be done without music as a finger play and choral speaking activity. When the children have learned it, they will enjoy singing the melody as they do the motions.

Put your left hand out, palm down, fingers together, thumb sticking out. Put your right hand on top of the left, palm down, thumb out. (See the fish with fins at his sides.) Wiggle your thumbs and make the fish swim by moving hands up and down in unison. Now make the fish swim and wiggle his fins at the same time. Open his mouth. Keep the hands together but drop the left hand fingers and raise the right hand fingers. Rub tummy.

Jack O'Lantern

Brennan

Blake

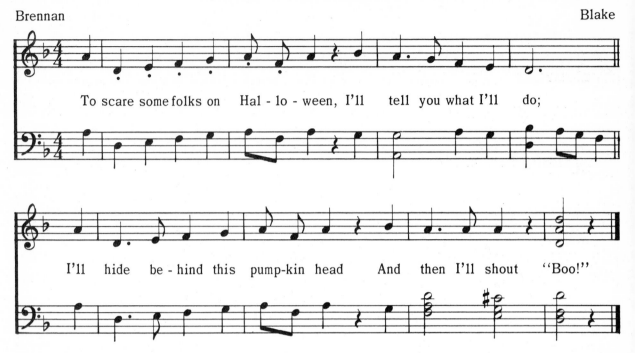

To scare some folks on Hal - lo - ween, I'll tell you what I'll do;

I'll hide be - hind this pump-kin head And then I'll shout "Boo!"

Words and music used by permission of The Willis Music Co.

1. Using a large pumpkin cutout do exactly as the song says.

2. One child may stand in front of the group to say "Boo!" at the right time from in back of the pumpkin head.

We have known many young retarded children who have made their first vocal response to this song. In any event, everyone will want a turn. Considerable self-control is required by those who are singing and not holding pumpkin faces not to say "Boo!"

Little Sally More

English Game Song

Lit - tle Sal - ly More, Sit - ting on the floor, Cry, Sal - ly, cry, cry, Wipe out your eye, Turn to the East, Turn to the West, Turn to the one that you like best.

1. A child sits or squats in the center of the circle pantomiming the actions and "Boo-hoo-ing" on "Cry, Sally, cry," as the rest of the group sings. The child rises after "Wipe out your eye" with eyes closed and one arm extended. Point right and left, and to the child who has the next turn.

2. Use the first name of children in your group - Little Susie More. If a boy - Mr. Robert More.

3. If you have a rocking chair you might make this "Little Sally Locker, Sitting in a rocker," or, "Mr. Johnny Trench, Sitting on a bench."

I Wish I Was

Traditional

I wish I was a bird up in a tree. I wish I was a bird up in a tree. If I were a bird up in a tree, I'd sing a song for you and me, I wish I was a bird up in a tree.

I wish I was a busy honey bee.
I'd make lots of honey for you and me.

I wish I was a shiny silver bell.
I'd go ding-dong, and ding-dong-dell.

I wish I was a monkey in a tree.
I'd make a funny face for you to see.

I wish I was a cow named Emmy Lou.
I'd moo, and moo, and moo at you.

1. Make up other verses to suit the occasion.
2. Make the motion or sound suggested in each verse at the end of each phrase.
   For instance: honey bee—bzzz, bzzzz.
3. Play a rhythm instrument at the same place at the end of each phrase.

Valentines

W.E.S.

Folk Song

Val - en - tines come when it's Val - en - tine's Day,

Val - en - tines pret - ty and Val - en - tines gay.

One came just now and it says, "I love you.

Please be my Val - en - tine. Can you guess who?"

La Jesucita

Mexican Folk Song

From listening to this folk song being played you will discover two melodies which may be called "A" and "B." Be sure that the children hear where each melody begins, then try these rhythm instrument activities.

1. Tap a steady rhythm with rhythm sticks during "A." Wait quietly during "B," and resume tapping when "A" returns.
2. Use sticks during "A," maracas or tambourine during "B." Tap lightly!
3. Same as above using both instruments on the repetition of "A."
4. Develop a simple dance to this music using one step for "A" and a different one for "B."

Santa Claus Is Coming

Adapted

Folk Song

Oh, San - ta Claus is com - ing, For Christ - mas Day, Oh,

San - ta Claus is com - ing, For Christ - mas Day!

I hear his sleighbells jingling.   He's brought a ball for Baby.
I hear him on the rooftop.   He's brought a shirt for Daddy.
He's coming down the chimney.   He's brought a dress for Mommy.
He's filling all the stockings.   He's going up the chimney.
He's brought a doll for Sister.   He's calling "Merry Christmas!"
He's brought a truck for Brother.

Using the names of the children in your group sing about the toys or gifts they want: "Oh, Johnny wants a cowboy suit, For Christmas Day," et cetera.

Look in the Mirror

D.R.G. - W.E.S.

Folk Tune Adapted

Do you see teeth clean and white?
Yes, I see teeth clean and white.
Do you see eyes shining bright?
Yes, I see eyes shining bright.
Eyes so bright, teeth so white,
Hair in place, nice clean face,
Children, children, look in the mirror,
Tell me, tell me what you see.

Do you see clothes straight and neat?
Yes, I see clothes straight and neat.
Are you trim from head to feet?
Yes, I'm trim from head to feet.
Head to feet, clothes are neat,
Eyes so bright, teeth so white,
Hair in place, nice clean face,
Children, children, look in the mirror,
And be proud of what you see!

* Autoharp accomp. in key of F.

"M" Is for Mary

D.R.G.

D.R.G.

"M" is for Mary, It's eas-y you see.

"M" is for Ma-ry, Now show it to me.

"M" is for Mary, I found it, you see,
"M" is for Mary, It's easy for me.

Presenting instructional material in a variety of ways appeals to all children, but is particularly helpful to retarded children. Chanted or sung, this little song can help vary the ways in which letters are presented and can help teach recognition of common objects and the development of a "sight" vocabulary.

1. Children's names on cards may be placed on a blackboard ledge. A duplicate card is shown to the child as the song is sung. The card is given to the child, and he finds the matching card. Later only the first letter of his name is on the card he receives. Still later, no card is given to use as a clue. The second verse is sung when the child brings back the right card.

2. The alphabet may be taught in this manner beginning with pictures of familiar objects. The initial letter or the complete object name may be on the picture card. Related groups of things may be used: fruits, vegetables, furniture, animals, et cetera.

3. The color names, number names, days, et cetera, may be presented in a similar manner.

4. Use pictures of objects needed for speech practice.

Merry Christmas to You

Traditional Melody

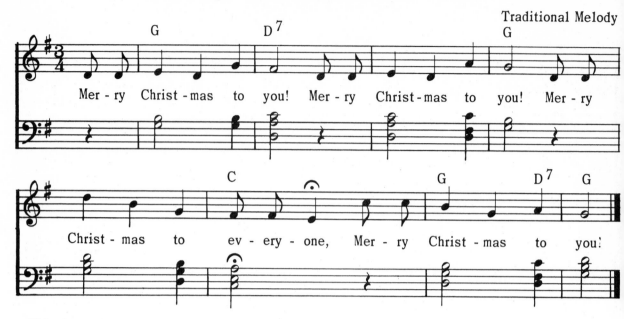

Mer - ry Christ - mas to you! Mer - ry Christ - mas to you! Mer - ry

Christ - mas to ev - ery - one, Mer - ry Christ - mas to you!

This familiar melody may be used in many ways for greetings and holiday wished:

Happy Easter to you!

Happy holidays to you!

If the group wishes to thank someone who has done something nice for them, they may sing, "We thank you very much"—or everybody, or the name of the individual.
And of course there is:

Good morning to you!
Good morning to you!
Good morning, ...
We're glad to see you.

Mildred J. Hill

Mother Loves Me

W. B. BRADBURY

Sing about Daddy, Grandma, and others who love us too.

My Little Pony

English Folk Song

1. Children walk in a circle for first four phrases. Gallop during the "Giddiaps," pull on the reins and come to a halt.

2. Substitute the name of your town or a town close by.

Noble Duke of York

English Game Song

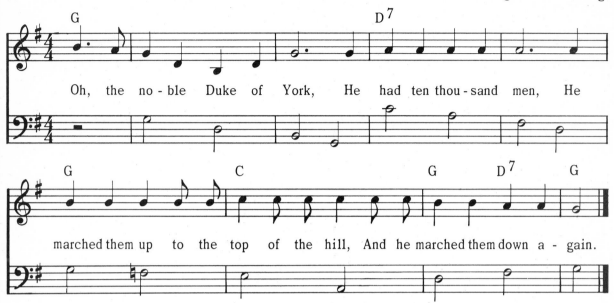

Oh, the no - ble Duke of York, He had ten thou - sand men, He marched them up to the top of the hill, And he marched them down a - gain.

Now when they were up they were up,
And when they were down they were down;
But when they were only halfway up,
They were neither up nor down.

1. This old favorite lends itself to finger-play exercise and body and arm movements. It helps to establish concepts of up, down, and halfway up.

Oh, the noble Duke of York,	*Hold up ten fingers and wiggle them.*
He had ten thousand men,	
He marched them up to the top of the hill,	*Use hands in ascending climbing motion.*
And he marched them down again.	*Use hands in descending motion.*
Now when they were up they were up,	*Hold arms over head on "up."*
And when they were down they were down,	*Drop arms toward floor on "down."*
But when they were only halfway up,	*Hold arms straight ahead.*
They were neither up nor down.	*Overhead on "up" and down toward floor on "down."*

2. When the children have learned this, use the song for body motions.

Oh, the noble Duke of York,	*Hold up ten fingers and wiggle them.*
He had ten thousand men,	
He marched them up to the top of the hill,	*Stand up gradually.*
And he marched them down again.	*Sit down gradually.*
Now when they were up they were up,	*Stand up quickly.*
And when they were down, they were down,	*Sit down quickly.*
But when they were only halfway up,	*Rise halfway from chair.*
They were neither up nor down.	*Stand up, sit down.*

Oh, Dear!

English Folk Song

Oh, dear, what can the mat-ter be? Oh, dear, what can the mat-ter be?
Look, look, here he comes back a-gain, Look, look, here he comes back a-gain,

Oh, dear, what can the mat-ter be? John-ny's so long at the store.
Look, look, here he comes back a-gain, John-ny is back from the store.

He prom-ised to bring me some pep-per-mint can-dy, He

prom-ised to bring me some pep-per-mint can-dy, He

82

prom - ised   to   bring   me   some   pep - per - mint   can - dy,

D.C.

when   he   comes   back   from   the   store!

1. Use the names of the children in your group. Talk about and decide what each child is going to bring from the store. In the beginning the teacher or leader may suggest things, but with practice the children will make their own suggestions. Pictures of various articles will help. You may need to phrase the suggestion to fit the rhythm—pretty red roses, cake for my birthday, shiny new bicycle, et cetera. Dramatize the song simply by having a child go to another part of the room—the store—and return at the right time in the music. Pictures or other objects may be placed in the ''store'' so that the child may bring back the right one.

2. Later you may decide on the kind of store Johnny will go to and select an article that would be found in that store. The note values of the last measure would change accordingly:

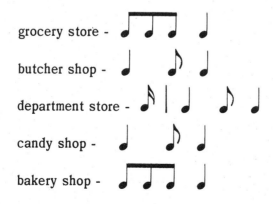

83

Our Flag

W.E.S.
W.E.S.

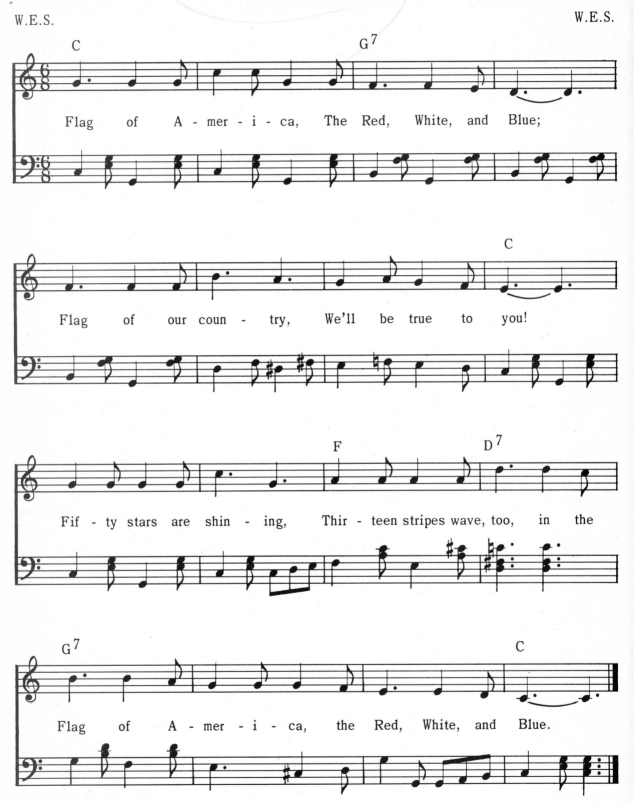

Flag of A - mer - i - ca, The Red, White, and Blue;

Flag of our coun - try, We'll be true to you!

Fif - ty stars are shin - ing, Thir - teen stripes wave, too, in the

Flag of A - mer - i - ca, the Red, White, and Blue.

Our March

Unknown

D.C. al FINE

This rhythmic tune lends itself to many activities. It may be used for marching, skipping, hopping, jumping, bending, rocking, swinging arms, et cetera.

One, Two, What Shall I Do?

W.E.S.   W.E.S.

Teacher: One, two, *Child:* One, two, *T.* What shall I do? *C.* What shall I do?

T. Three, four, *C.* Three, four, *T.* Tap on the floor. *C.* Tap on the floor.

T. Five, six, *C.* Five, six, *T.* Play on the sticks, *C.* Play on the sticks.

T. Sev - en, eight, *C.* Sev - en, eight, *T.* Hold them out straight, *C.* Hold them out straight.

T. Nine, ten, *C.* Nine, ten, *T.* Play them a - gain! *C.* Play them a - gain!

Using either fingers or sticks, do just as the song says. The teacher or leader sings and does the action first. The children must wait to sing and do the action.

Pointing

D.R.G.

W.E.S.

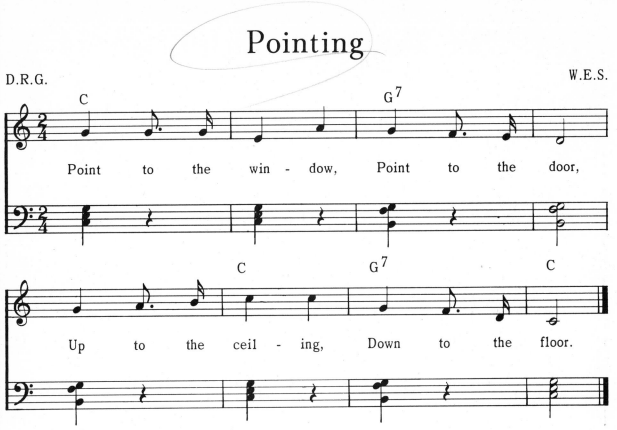

Point to the win-dow, Point to the door,

Up to the ceil-ing, Down to the floor.

Point to your head, now
Point to your knee,
Point to your elbow,
Now point to me.

Point to a table
Point to a chair,
Point to a friend of yours
Sitting over there.

Later, arrange color cards in different sequences and sing:

Please point to yellow,
Next point to blue,
Now point to red, and green,
That's fine! Thank you.

For the child with limited or no speech, pointing is often one of the earliest means of communication. Pointing can be one way of beginning instruction or training in terms of seeing likenesses and differences and a means of assessing comprehension in many ways.

Put Your Finger in the Air

Woody Guthrie
Additional verses by D. R. G.

Woody Guthrie

Put your fin - ger in the air, in the air; Put your fin - ger in the air, in the air. Put your fin - ger in the air, put your fin - ger in the air, Put your fin - ger in the air, in the air.

Put your finger on your head, on your head,
Put your finger on your head, on your head,
Put your finger on your head, tell me is it green or red?
Put your finger on your head, on your head.

On your nose . . . And feel how the cold wind blows.

On your shoe . . . And leave it a day or two.

On your finger . . . And your finger on your finger.

On your chin . . . That's where the food slips in.

On your cheek . . . And leave it about a week.

On your knee . . . All together, one, two, three.

On your wrist . . . Give it a little twist.

On your shoulder . . . Leave it there till you get older.

On your hip . . . Just your tiny fingertip.

On your neck . . . Now let's all double check.

On your tummy . . . Oh, my, you look so funny!

On your ear . . . Now aren't you a dear!

On your back . . . I can see you're on the track.

This is a very active fun song with the children and the leader performing the motions indicated.

Rig-a-Jig-Jig

English Folk Song

way we go, hi - ho, hi - ho, hi - ho!

1. Children are seated or standing in a circle. One child walks around the outside of the circle as the group sings the first part of the song. The child chooses a partner to skip (or run lightly) with him during "Rig-a-jig-jig." The child chosen then walks alone, and the game proceeds as before. Substitute the name of the child in the song—"As David was walking down the street."

2. The children in the circle may "walk" their hands on their knees as they sing. Make the hands "skip" or "gallop" on the chorus.

3. Each child may decide to go down the street a different way such as hopping, sliding, running, et cetera. Always skip on the chorus. Vary the tempo on the piano or autoharp to suit the action.

4. Using rhythm sticks, tap on the floor with alternate hands during the walking part. Bring the sticks up quickly and tap them in the melody rhythm during the chorus.

5. Use sticks or woodblock on the verse, tambourine or bells on the chorus.

The Seasons

Traditional Melody

What can you do in the win - ter - time, win - ter - time,

win - ter - time? What can you do in the

win - ter - time? In the win - ter of the year?

I shovel snow in the wintertime, wintertime, wintertime.

I ride my sled—build a fort—skate on ice, et cetera.

What can you do in the warm springtime?
I dig the ground—plant the seeds—clean the yard.

What can you do in the summertime?
I cut the grass—weed the garden—paint the fence.

What can you do in the autumntime?
I rake the leaves—pick the fruit—dig potatoes.

Another version:

What do you like in the wintertime?
  I like to slide—to sled—the snow—the ice.

What do you like in the warm springtime?
  I like the birds—the flowers—to play—jumping rope.

What do you like in the summertime?
  I like the sun—to swim—the beach—playing ball.

What do you like in the autumn time?
  I like to hike—the leaves—the apples—Halloween.

Skip to My Lou

Traditional Melody

skip to my Lou, Skip to my Lou, my dar - ling.

1. As a circle game, the children stand or are seated in a circle. One child walks around the outside of the circle as the group sings, "Choose a friend . . . ." The child chooses a partner, and they skip or run lightly around the circle as the group sings the chorus. The child chosen then walks alone, and the game proceeds as before.

2. Using the words below, the children stand in a circle facing a partner and pantomime the action. During the chorus, partners take hands and skip or run lightly in a clockwise direction. Children again face partners and continue with the next verse.

> Washing on Monday, Lou, Lou, Lou. (Sing 3 times.)
> Skip to my Lou, my darling.
> Lou, Lou, skip to my Lou. (Sing 3 times.)
> Skip to my Lou, my darling.
>
> Ironing on Tuesday
>
> Sewing on Wednesday
>
> Sweeping on Thursday
>
> Scrubbing on Friday
>
> Cooking on Saturday
>
> Praying on Sunday

3. Same as above, except at the end of the chorus the inner circle stands still and the outer circle moves ahead to new partners. In this way each child has a new partner for each new day. This is difficult for many retarded children and should not be attempted too soon.

Sounds I Hear

W.E.S.   W.E.S.

Hands are for clap - ping, clap - pi - ty, clap!

Hands are for clap - ing, clap - pi - ty, clap! Clap - pi - ty, clap,

Clap - pi - ty, clap,   Clap,   clap,   Clap - pi - ty, clap!

Words and music copyright © 1965 by Abingdon Press.

Feet are for tapping, tappity, tap.

Drums are for banging, bangity, bang.

Bells are for ringing, ringity, ring.

Sticks are for clicking, clickity, click.

Children play or pretend to play the instruments indicated. Wait for the right words before playing.

98

Take Away Song

D.R.G.
W.E.S.

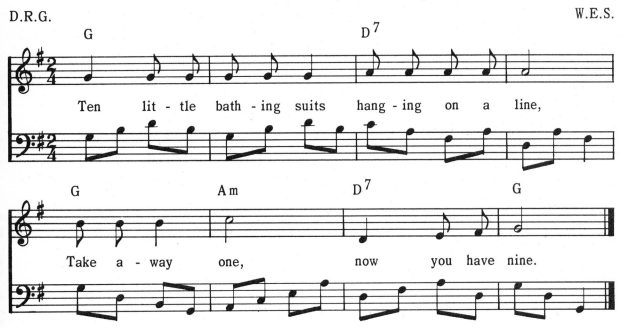

Ten lit - tle bath - ing suits hang - ing on a line,
Take a - way one, now you have nine.

Nine little lollipops standing up so straight,
Take away one, now you have eight.
Eight little bluebirds flying up to heaven,
Take away one, now you have seven.
Seven little children playing rhythm sticks,
Take away one, now you have six.
Six little bumble bees buzzing 'round the hive
Take away one, now you have five.
Five little puppies playing on the floor,
Take away one, now you have four.
Four little apples hanging on a tree,
Take away one, now you have three.
Three little Indians, each in his canoe,
Take away one, now you have two.
Two little swimmers sitting in the sun,
Take away one, now you have one.
One little cowboy shooting with a gun,
Take him away, now you have none.

1. Children hold up both hands with fingers erect. Beginning with the thumb, each time one is taken away fold or bend one finger down, keeping the others erect until there are none left.

2. In a class situation, ten children may be selected to stand in front of the group. Each time one is taken away the child on the extreme left returns to his seat.

3. Simple cutouts of paper may be used on the flannel board.

4. Each child may hold a large number. As the song is sung he puts his number on the flannel board or easel at the right time.

Stodola Pumpa

D.R.G. - W.E.S.

Czech Folk Tune

Blue is the sky, the sun is shin-ing too, Let's take a walk, I'll go a-long with you. Blue is the sky, the sun is shin-ing too, Let's take a walk, I'll go a-long with you. HEY!

CHORUS

Sto-do-la, sto-do-la, sto-do-la pum-pa,

sto - do - la pum - p a, sto - do - la pum - pa, Sto - do - la, sto - do - la,

sto - do - la pum - pa, sto - do - la pum - pa, pum, pum, pum.

We must be home before the sun goes down,
Let's turn around and walk right back to town.

1. On the chorus clap once for each "stodola" and slap knees twice on "pumpa."
2. Use this as a group walking activity. Children take partners and walk hand in hand, or arm in arm, singing the verse. Face each other on "Hey!" Clap hands on "stodola" partner's hands on "pumpa" pattycake fashion. Walk "home" on the second verse.
3. Use rhythm sticks, tapping them together on "stodola" on the floor on "pumpa."
4. Choose two different instruments, one for "stodola," one for "pumpa," remembering to play them at the right time.

This Old Man

Traditional

This old man, He played one, He played knick-knack on my thumb.

Knick-knack paddy-whack, give the dog a bone, This old man came rol-ling home.

2–shoe	5–side	8–gate
3–knee	6–sticks	9–spine
4–floor	7–up in heaven	10–once again

1. As a game, tap thumb, knee, floor, et cetera. Clap on "paddy-whack," pantomime "give the dog a bone," and then roll hands.

2. All children play sticks on "knick-knack."

3. Each child plays one verse using different instruments. Try to play:

Tap: x x x x   x   x
Sing: This old man, He played one,

Tap: x x   x   x   x x   x
Sing: He played knick-knack on my thumb.
   (Count 1, 2, 3 as you play.)

4. Vary the chorus by using different instruments such as: "Knick-knack, paddy-whack"—tambourine; "Give the dog a bone"—wood block; "This old man came rolling home"—trill triangle.

This Way, Valerie

Southern Folk Game

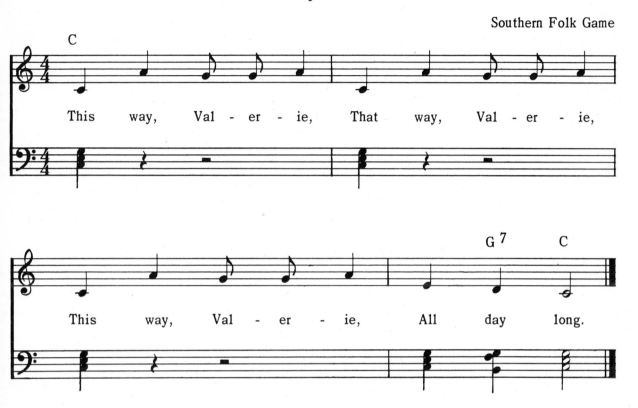

This way, Val - er - ie, That way, Val - er - ie,

This way, Val - er - ie, All day long.

Skip, Miss Valerie, All day long.

Here comes another one,
Just like the other one,
Here comes another one,
All day long.

1. Form two lines of partners facing each other. Take hands.

This way, Valerie,	*Point right heels.*
That way, Valerie,	*Point left heels.*
This way, Valerie,	*Point right heels.*
All day long.	*Quick heel change, left, right, left.*

2. "Miss Valerie" skips (or hops, dances, whirls, et cetera) between the lines to the other end.

3. "Another one"—Miss Valerie's partner—does the same action down the line. The game starts again with the next couple.

4. Use the names of the children in the group—Mister Johnny, Miss Susie, et cetera. If the children are not sure of right and left, have them start with the foot nearest the door or window.

Tinga Layo

Calypso Song

Ting - a Lay - o,   Come, lit - tle don - key, come.   Ting-a

Lay - o,   Come, lit - tle don - key, come.   Come.

1. My don -key walk, my don -key talk, My don -key eat with a knife and fork.
2. My don -key eat, my don -key sleep, My don -key kick with his two hind feet.

1. Tinga   *Clap twice.*
   lay   *With the arms make two circles up and out. Complete the circles in time to*
   o   *Clap.*

Then clap the rhythm of ''Come, little donkey, come.'' Slap the knees in rhythm of ''My donkey walk,'' et cetera.

2. With a triangle or tambourine tap twice and then trill on ''lay.'' Use a different instrument, such as a wood block or sticks, on ''Come, little donkey, come.'' Use maracas for the last section.

Who Am I?

W.E.S.
W.E.S.

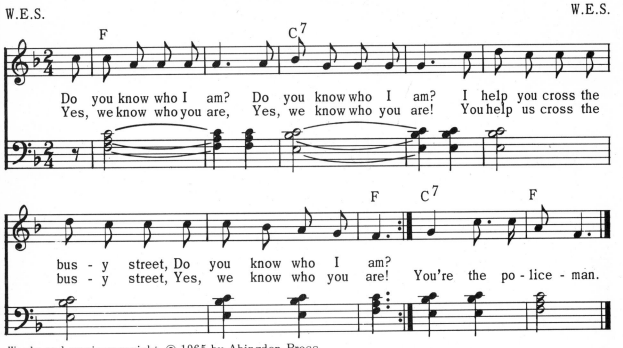

Do you know who I am? Do you know who I am? I help you cross the
Yes, we know who you are, Yes, we know who you are! You help us cross the

bus - y street, Do you know who I am? Youʼre the po - lice - man.
bus - y street, Yes, we know who you are! Youʼre the po - lice - man.

Make up verses for people who help us:

> I help you grow up well and strong . . . the doctor.
>
> I help you learn so many things . . . the teacher.
>
> I take you to your school each day . . . the bus driver.
>
> I answer evʼry fire alarm . . . the fireman.
>
> I bring you cards and letters too . . . the postman.

Or family and friends:

> I tuck you into bed each night . . . my Mother.
>
> I go to work for you each day . . . my Father.
>
> I wave to you when you go by . . . the neighbors.

Or people who come now and then:

> I ring my bell as I go by . . . the ice-cream man.
>
> I fill your stockings full of toys . . . Santa.

What Will You Do Now?

As sung by M. RAYMOND

Hel - lo, Sal - ly, How are you? How are you?

How are you? Hel - lo, Sal - ly, How are you?

W.E.S.

What will you do now?

1. Children sit or stand in a circle with the leader in the center. The circle sings:

> Hello, teacher, how are you, how are you, how are you?
> Hello, teacher, how are you? What will you do now?

The leader will do some rhythmic activity which is imitated by all in the circle. A child is then chosen to stand in the middle. The game proceeds as before, substituting the name of the child in the song. Encourage each child to do something different. The leader may help by whispering to the child, "Touch your toes," "Slap your knees," "Roll your hands," et cetera.

2. A box of rhythm instruments may be placed in the circle, and the child in the center may select an instrument to play a solo during the second part.

When Johnny Comes Marching Home

Words (alt.) and music by
PATRICK S. GILMORE

When John - ny comes march - ing home a - gain, Hur-

rah! Hur - rah! We'll give him a heart - y wel - come then, Hur-

rah! Hur - rah! We'll march a - long with our heads held high, We'll

all sa - lute as the flag goes by And we'll give a

cheer   when   John - ny   comes   march - ing   home!

1. Use this song for marching with emphasis on posture, marching—not stamping—in time to the music, and swinging the arms easily.

2. Try the following rhythm-instrument activities:

    (a) Listen to the introduction. Clap when the melody starts. Clap a steady 1, 2, not the melody rhythm.

    (b) Listen to the introduction. Play sticks or drum in a steady 1, 2, rhythm. Stop at the end of the melody. Wait for the interlude before playing the song again.

    (c) Listen to the introduction. Play sticks in the melody rhythm.

    (d) Play the 1, 2, rhythm on the drum, the melody rhythm on the sticks.

Isn't It Fun?

W.E.S.

Traditional Melody

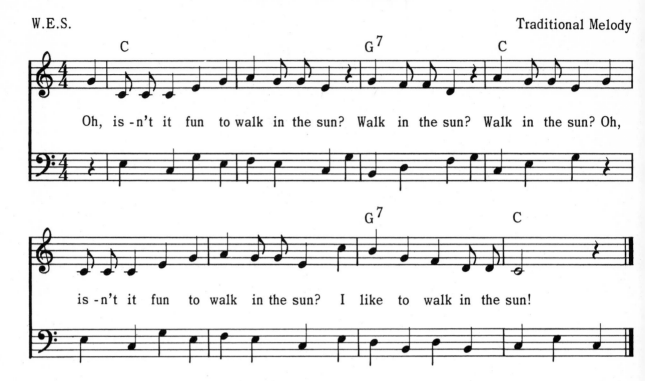

Isn't it fun to walk in the rain?

Isn't it fun walk in the snow?

Isn't it fun to walk in the leaves?

1. Dramatize the song by walking in various ways. Then add other kinds of walk such as:

Isn't it fun to walk like a clown, cat, bear, duck, ghost.

Isn't it fun to walk to the store, to school, to church.

2. Encourage the children to suggest something that is fun to do. The group can sing as one child does the action. The teacher or leader may help the child by suggesting something that is fun such as:

Isn't it fun to tap on the floor, knock on the door, slide on the ice, play in the snow, dig in the sand, et cetera.

3. Another approach might be to have a child act out something that is fun. When the group guesses what it is they sing, ''We think it's fun to . . . .''

This song lends itself to introducing and understanding many abstract concepts, action words, and in associating with words or sounds some of the things the children like to do.

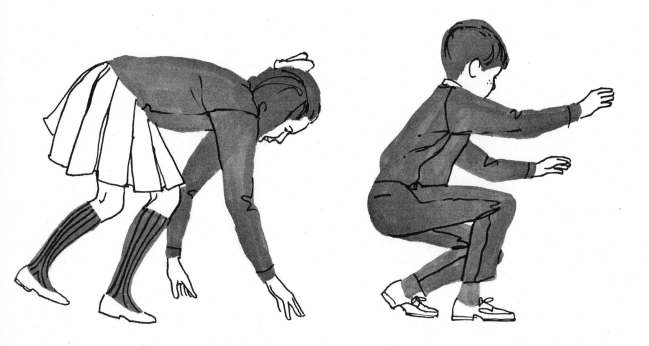

Winter Song

Marguery J. Saxe   Marguery J. Saxe

Let's pull out our mit - tens, but - ton up our coats,

Wrap a scarf so snug - ly a - round our throats.

Put our boots and hats on, Now we're read - y for snow.

O - pen up the door and out we go!

III
SIMPLE FOLK DANCING

There are logical reasons for including dance experiences in the curriculum for retarded children. We are concerned with developing better locomotor activity. With music, the rhythmic response is better controlled. Music provides a stimulus that helps children to walk, march, run, hop, jump. bend, twist, turn, et cetera, and to express ideas with their bodies. Through folk dancing, children progress from fundamental movements to more complex ones. We do not teach measure and beat to retarded children in a formal way, but their bodies can learn these things by doing them. Evidence of growth will be clearly indicated in their response to tempo, accent, beat, et cetera.

Circle singing games should be well established before simple folk dancing is introduced. Severely retarded children cannot, in most instances, learn line formations or squares effectively for dancing, certainly not before they have had a great deal of experience in basic rhythmic body movements. This does not mean that children must be denied the satisfactions of dancing, however. Folk dancing can be presented in such a manner as to guarantee minimal success in initial efforts which can later lead to improvement and growth.

In the initial teaching, it may help for the teacher to take individual children as partners and to demonstrate to the rest of the group, but generally it will be best to have everyone try the dance at the same time. In the beginning it will help to pair a more able child with a less able one, but after the action is learned, children of equal ability should be paired so that they may fully enjoy the fun and spontaneity of the dance.

To begin, place couples around the room and indicate the direction that skipping or running on tiptoe will take. A long bench or table placed in the center of the room provides a guide around which to move and helps the children to avoid collisions and the herding together that frequently takes place. All action is shared with one's partner. The only group action required is the moving of all couples in a clockwise direction.

Do not be a perfectionist; the children will gain skill unevenly. Claps and bows may not be in time or correct in number, but improvement will be noted as the children come to understand what to do and become comfortable in knowing what is expected. Remember that children who have not developed stamina will tire easily or may become overstimulated when activities are new. Fifteen or twenty minutes of active dancing is quite enough for a beginning period. This activity should be followed by a rest period or a quiet game. A brief dancing period every day will yield better results than a more prolonged period once a week.

Bleking

Swedish

With a one, and two, and one, two, three, With a

one, and two, and one, two, three, With a one, and two, and

one, two, three, With a one, and two, and one, two, three.

One foot, oth - er foot, et cetera.

The words given here are not meant to be sung but to be chanted to help with the timing of the first step.

Children face partners and hold both hands. Hop on left foot, put right heel forward touching the floor. Reverse feet. Continue in this pattern—one, two; one, two, three.

Drop partner's outside hand and move in a clockwise direction with a heavy stamp-hop, alternating left and right feet in time to the music.

Children's Polka

German

Children face partners, holding both hands.

Oh, slide, and slide, and stamp, stamp, stamp,   *Two side-steps; three stamps. (Four times.)*

Your knees, your hands, and one, two, three,   *Slap knees, clap hands, clap partner's hands three times pattycake fashion.*

Oh, shake your finger, shake your finger,   *One hand on hip, shake finger of other hand at partner.*

Turn around and stamp, stamp, stamp!   *Turn independently, three stamps.*

Chimes of Dunkirk

French

Oh, stamp, and stamp, and stamp! Then clap, and clap, and

clap! Now turn your-self a - round in a cir - cle,

stamp, stamp, stamp! Tra, la, la, la, la, la! Tra,

la, la, la, la, la! Tra, la, la, la, la la! Tra, la, la, la, la, la!

1. Children stand in a large circle. Do the actions indicated. Join hands and rotate on chorus.

2. Children face partners and do actions indicated. Take partner's hand and skip in a large circle during the chorus.

Czardas

Hungarian

Slide, and slide, slide the oth-er way, Slide, and slide,

slide, we're here to stay. Walk in-to the mid-dle and you

take a lit-tle bow, Back, and back, Back, stamp, stamp.

1. Children form one large circle. Hold hands throughout the dance.
Take four side-steps, then reverse direction for four more side-steps. Taking very small steps, walk in toward the center and bow. Step backward bringing the feet together at each step for three steps. Stamp twice. Repeat.

2. Couples face each other holding both hands. Take side-steps, four in each direction. Drop one hand and face center for other steps. Repeat.

Dance of Greeting

Danish

Clap, clap, bow, Clap, clap, bow, Stamp, stamp, and turn your-self a - round.

Go on your tip - py - toe, your tip - py - tip - py - tip - toe,

Go on your tip - py - toe, your tip - py - tip - py - toe.

Children face each other and do the actions indicated.
Take hands and move lightly on tiptoe in a clockwise direction.

120

Shoemaker's Dance

Danish

Children face partners.

Wind, wind, wind the thread,	*Roll hands around each other.*
And zip! And zip!	*Pull imaginary needle upward.*
And tap, tap, tap!	*Pound fists together and stamp one foot.*
Tiptoe, tiptoe 'round the room.	*Join hands and tiptoe gracefully.*

The Gay Musician

German

clap, clap, here, And a clap, clap, there, With a clap, clap, clap, clap, clap.

Children walk with partners in a circle clockwise. Hold partner's hand.

Oh, I'm a gay musician,	*Step, step, step, heel forward.*
I come from far away.	*Step, step, step, heel forward.*
Oh, I'm a gay musician,	*Step, step, step, heel forward.*
I come from far away.	*Step, step, step, heel forward.*
With a clap, clap, here,	*Face away from each other, clap three times near the floor.*
And a clap, clap, there,	*Turn toward each other, clap three times near the floor.*
With a clap, clap, here,	*Repeat as above.*
And a clap, clap, there,	
Slide, Johnny, slide, oh,	*Take both hands, four side-step slides.*
Slide, Johnny, slide, oh,	
With a clap, clap, here,	*Repeat as above on claps.*
And a clap, clap, there,	
With a clap, clap, clap, clap, clap.	*Gradually slower on last five claps.*

How Do You Do, My Partner?

American Folk Dance

How do you do, my partner, How do you do to-day? Will you dance in the cir - cle? I will show you the way. Tra, la, la, la, la, la, la, la, et cetera.

1. Children face partners standing in a large circle.

How do you do, my partner,   *Boys bow, girls curtsy.*
How do you do, today?   *Repeat.*
Will you dance in a circle?   *Link arms and circle in place.*
I will show you the way.
Tra, la, la, et cetera.   *Join inside hands and skip or run lightly around the room in a large circle.*

124

2. Children face partners standing in a large circle. Sing the first two lines and bow or curtsy as above. The leader sings the next lines which give the cue for the rest of the action:

Will you give me your hand?	*Take partner's hand.*
And we'll circle this way.	*Circle in place.*
Will you give me your hand?	*Take partner's hand.*
We'll go skipping away.	*Skip around the room.*
Will you give me your hands?	*Take hands.*
And we'll circle this way.	*Circle in place.*
Will you give me your hands?	*Take hands.*
We'll go sliding away.	*Slide around room.*
Will you give me your arm?	*Take arms.*
And we'll circle this way.	*Circle in place.*
Will you give me your arm?	*Take arms.*
We will promenade away.	*Promenade around room.*

Alternating the action during the chorus with circling in place then circling around the room makes for better control and is less tiring to the children.

La Raspa

W.E.S.

Mexican

Oh, hear our danc-ing feet! The mus-ic is bright and gay; Oh,

hear the hap-py beat of cast-a-nets as they play. play.

La, la, la, la, la, la, la, la, et cetera.

1. Clap hands in time with the first part of the song. Pretend to play the piano while singing the "la's."

2. Stamp feet for first part. Roll hands on the second part.

3. As a circle game, alternate clapping and hopping on the first part. Join hands and circle on the second part.

4. With partners facing each other and holding hands, hop from one foot to the other pointing the heels. Link arms and skip or run lightly around each other during the second part.

5. Tap rhythm sticks on the first part. On the second part tap the floor, or rotate sticks around each other, or pretend they are maracas and shake them alternately in the air.

6. Tap a tambourine three times, then shake for two measures. Repeat three times. Use maracas or castanets for the second part.

The Minuet

Mozart

Step, step, and step, and point your toe. Step, step, and step, and

point your oth - er toe. Step, step, and step, and point your toe. And

bow, the min - u - et. Step, step, and step, and turn a - round,

Step, step, and step, and turn a - round. Step, and step, and step and

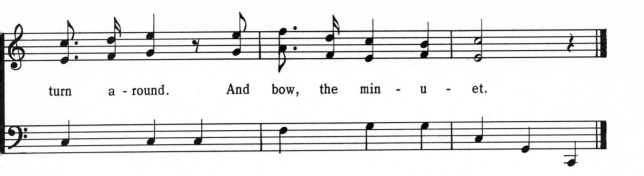

turn a - round. And bow, the min - u - et.

This definite change in tempo is a good test to see if the children hear and respond to tempo in music.

Children stand beside partners. Hold inner hands aloft. Walk gracefully in time with the music.

Step, step, and step, and point your toe.   *Three steps, point outer feet.*
Step, step, and step, and point your other toe, *Three steps, point inner feet.*
Step, step, and step, and point your toe, *Three steps, point outer feet.*
And bow, the minuet.   *Slow bow and curtsy,*

Step, step, and step, and turn around. *Three steps, drop hands to turn (Three times.)*
And bow, the minuet.

Turn, turn, and turn, and point your toe. *Hold hands and turn in place (Three times.)*
And bow, the minuet.

Step, step, and step, and bow,   *Three steps, bow away from partner.*
Back, back, and back, and bow,   *Three steps back, bow.*
Step, step, and step, and bow,   *As above.*
And bow, the minuet.

Shoo Fly!

American

Shoo, fly! Don't both - er me. Shoo, fly! Don't both - er me.

Shoo, fly! Don't both - er me. For I be - long to

some - bod - y. I feel, I feel, I feel like a morn - ing

star! I feel, I feel, I feel like a morn - ing star!

1. Children stand in one large circle holding hands.

Shoo, fly! Don't bother me.	*Step in toward center.*
Shoo, fly! Don't bother me.	*Step back.*
Shoo, fly! Don't bother me.	*Step in.*
For I belong to somebody.	*Step back.*
I feel, I feel, I feel like a morning star!	*Circle rotates clockwise.*
I feel, I feel, I feel like a morning star!	*Circle rotates counterclockwise.*

2. Partners face each other.

Shoo, fly! Don't bother me.	*Make a "Shoo!" motion. (Three times.)*
For I belong to somebody.	*Take hands or link arms and rotate.*
I feel, et cetera.	*Take hands and promenade.*

3. Partners face each other holding hands.

Shoo, fly! Don't bother me, et cetera.	*Step in toward center and back as in No. 1 above.*
I feel, I feel, et cetera.	*Take hands or link arms and rotate in place in a clockwise direction.*
I feel, I feel, et cetera.	*Reverse to counterclockwise direction.*

IV
OTHER MUSICAL ACTIVITIES

Using the Record Player

A careful selection of phonograph records can enrich and add to the scope of the music program in all areas.   See "Supplementary Materials," pp. 137.)

A record player can be carried to the playroom or gymnasium and is basic to an outdoor recreation program, such as a camp. The retarded child may have his own record player at home and may develop his own collection of records which he enjoys alone or shares with others. Using a record player frees you (the teacher or leader) to assist and participate directly with the children. It enables you to be a model for children to imitate and to provide a focal point for their attention.

Your record player is an extremely valuable piece of equipment. It should be durable, easy to operate, and have good volume and tone production. Insist on a manually operated machine! Avoid automatic changers which may break down with rugged use or may hinder timing by slowing transfers to various speeds and making it inconvenient to place the pickup on desired bands, et cetera.,

Many portable record players have a +5 −15 per cent speed regulator, which means that on any standard 78, 45, or 33 1/3 rpm setting the recorded speed may be slowed down. Wisely used, this enables you to play music that ordinarily might be too fast for retarded children. For example, when teaching a dance or other activity you may begin at a reduced speed and then gradually increase the speed to the original rpm when the action of the activity has become familiar. Use this regulator cautiously as distortion can result, but more important, spontaneity and enjoyment may be sacrificed by playing everything too slowly. Change of speed will, of course, cause a variation in pitch.

Naturally, good equipment should be used properly if it is to last. This is particularly true of the pickup, which is most often damaged. Be sure to have the correct setting on both turntable and pickup for the record to be played. Place stickers on your records with the rpm marked in large numbers. Avoid unnecessary handling and scratching of records. Children should not be

allowed to operate the record player. Correct operation becomes habit if thought is given to the consistent care needed to keep equipment operating efficiently.

How to Use the Autoharp

The autoharp is a simple instrument that enables one to add a rhythmic chordal accompaniment to songs with a minimum of practice.

Playing the instrument in the position described below has been found to produce better tone and freedom of motion although it is at variance with the directions usually included with the autoharp.

The instrument may be held on the lap or placed on a table with the strings going toward the left.

The "buttons" are arranged for the left hand. For example, in the key of F, place the left index finger on the button labeled F-maj. The other two chords frequently occurring in that key, C-sev. and B♭-maj., will then fall under the second and third fingers. The same is true of other keys. Always press the bars down firmly, one at a time, so that no strings other than those in the chord desired may be heard.

Cross the right hand over the left hand to strum the strings, from the heavy longer strings to the thinner, shorter ones. Most people prefer to use their fingernails to strum, although a variety of picks will be included with the autoharp. It is desirable to strum rhythmically in the meter of the song to be sung, not following the rhythm of the melody. For example, if a song has two beats to a measure, strum evenly 1, 2, 1, 2, at first.

2 beats F   F   F   F
Choose your partner, Skip to my Lou,
C7   C7   C7   C7
Choose your partner, Skip to my Lou,
F   F   F   F
Choose your partner, Skip to my Lou,
C7   C7   F F
Skip to my Lou, my darling.

Later a rhythmic pattern may be used for variety such as:

The Use of Percussion Instruments

We have talked about the child's continuing need to learn to listen and to improve coordination. Rhythm or percussion instruments can contribute appreciably to these learnings. Percussion instruments delight children of all ages. As they improve in skill many avenues of enriched musical experience and self-expression are opened to them. Playing a rhythm instrument leads to an awareness of rhythm, which may lead naturally to rhythmic body movements which are necessary in the development of basic physical skills. Most retarded children can easily learn to play a variety of percussion instruments and enjoy doing so.

The formal study of rhythm and use of percussion is limitless and complex. We are concerned here, however, with developing simple basic skills in a broad way that will contribute to auditory training, coordination, and the pleasure of achievement, as well as musical development. Rhythm activities can and should begin on a very simple level and be slowly developed. When children have mastered the activities presented here, you will find many other ways to use percussion instruments to add variety and interest to your program—for example, in storytelling and dramatics.

Every class should have a basic set of top quality, commercially made instruments. These are musical instruments and the quality of tone is most important in their introduction and use. Good instruments are more durable and yield better and more pleasing effects.

A basic set of instruments should include rhythm sticks for each child, a variety of wood blocks (clave-tone, guiro, chinotone), triangles, tambourines, cymbals, wrist bells, and at least one drum. Single-frame tambourines will give the best service. Brass cymbals produce the best sound. Other instruments that are useful for many effects are finger cymbals, sandblocks, maracas, and claves. A variety of beaters, soft and hard, aids in the exploration of the various instruments and their possibilities.

It is best to introduce each rhythm instrument separately and to use it until each child is familiar with its sound and with the method of playing it. Later, combinations of instruments may be used. In general, it is wise not to combine more than two or three instruments in any one activity. This will vary, of course, with your group and their abilities. It is not necessary that each child play with every selection. In singing activities many will sing while others add instruments.

Eye-hand coordination is often poor in retarded children, as in many small children. Tapping against something offers a control and makes for better rhythm. Therefore, best results are obtained by playing the instruments with a motion as nearly like clapping as possible. Instruments that would appear to need the use of only one hand, such as jingle sticks, wrist bells, et cetera, should be tapped against the palm of the free hand.

<u>Sticks</u> should be available for every child. They should be used as a beginning instrument as the tone is light and the children are more able to hear the music they are accompanying. The motion used is closest to clapping, and it is assumed that the class has had much experience in clapping to music. Sticks may tap each other, the floor, or the air.

<u>Woodblocks</u> vary in sound according to size and construction. They are held in one hand and struck with a mallet on the side, halfway between the slots. They are excellent for the effect of trotting horses, clocks, woodpeckers, et cetera. The guiro-tone block makes a most satisfactory ''Quack'' when the grooves are scraped with the stick end of the mallet.

<u>Tambourines</u> may be tapped with the fingers or fist. They may also be shaken by a rapid wrist (not arm) movement.

<u>Triangles</u> should be held by a knob or string using the thumb and two fingers. Hold the string as close to the instrument as possible without touching it. It is struck with a metal striker on the inside of the horizontal bar. The tone varies with the weight and size of the instrument and the intensity with which it is struck. Since the lighter triangles are apt to spin around or sway when struck, the heavier ones are more suitable for young children. A trill is produced by rotating the striker quickly inside the triangle.

<u>Wrist Bells</u> give the best results when placed on one hand and hands are clapped together. As these instruments are hard to control it is best to use them only at times when a bell sound is necessary.

<u>Bell Sticks</u> may be tapped against another bell stick or a rhythm stick.

<u>Cymbals</u> are brought together with a sliding motion rather than straight together. One hand moves up as the other goes down. One cymbal may be struck with a soft mallet for a gong effect.

<u>Drums</u> are of many types. Those with a handle are held in one hand and struck with a hard or soft mallet. Others are meant to be held under the arm and played with the fingers or a mallet.

Experimentation with percussion instruments is a worthwhile activity. It is invaluable in satisfying children's curiosity and also in discovering the range of tone of each instrument and the manner of playing that produces the most pleasing results. Never let exploration become chaos, however.

Remember that in these rhythm activities the important first learnings are self-control, knowing when to play, and when to stop.

When children have become familiar with standard rhythm instruments, the construction of additional instruments of their own opens a fruitful source of handicraft. Most books on handicraft and books on rhythmic activities have sections on making rhythm instruments. It is an area that can be as simple or complex as the children's abilities permit. For example, the most retarded child can help to sand dowels for rhythm sticks, etc. The opportunities for learning and the psychological benefits to a child who values something that is his because he has made it are established and need not be elaborated here. Remember, when planning such projects, the importance of pleasing sound or effect and the proper playing of pupil-made instruments.

Varied Music Activities

Singing may be varied by humming or whistling the tune from time to time. With either activity it is a good idea for the teacher to keep the melody clear by playing it or by singing "la" as the children hum or whistle.

The humazoo, a simple plastic version of the old kazoo, is inexpensive and provides another change in sound. Children who make little or no attempt to sing will often try to "play" this little instrument and, therefore, find themselves singing. Many teachers find this tooting instrument a valuable aid in teaching certain speech sounds.

Stepbells (bells arranged on tiny stairs) and songbells (bells arranged like a xylophone) are also within the abilities of many retarded children. Some will pick out tunes they know. Scale songs are easy to play.

Resonator bells or tuned bell blocks are mounted separately. A child holds the one bell he is to play. In many songs where a certain note is repeated in a rhythmic sequence several times, the bell sound adds to the song. For instance, "G" could be played four times at the beginning of each phrase in "Amaryllis" (p. 24).

If there is a piano in the room, children will learn respect for it if they are allowed to "play" it in the right way. All children may start a song if the beginning note is marked in some way. Use a tiny star for a patriotic song, a bird sticker for a spring song, et cetera. A few children may be able to pick out simple tunes that they know if an octave, C - C, is framed in some way.

SUPPLEMENTARY MATERIALS

Books

The kindergarten and primary grade books of all the basic music series include songs, singing games, and other materials suitable for use with retarded children. This book should have resulted in establishing criteria for the selection of such material. Listed below are the primary grade books of each series as well as a few other helpful collections.

Basic Series

Berg, Richard C., et al. Music for Young Americans ("ABC Music Series," Books 1 and 2.) New York: American Book Company, 1959, 1963.

McConathy, Osbourne, et al. Experiences in Music for First Grade Children. ("New Music Horizons.") New York: Silver Burdett Company, 1949.

_____. Music for Early Childhood. ("New Music Horizons.") New York: Silver Burdett Company, 1952.

_____. "New Music Horizons," Book 2. New York: Silver Burdett Company, 1953.

Mursell, James Lockhart, et al. Music in Our Town. ("Music for Living.") New York: Silver Burdett Company, 1956.

_____. Music Through the Day. ("Music for Living.") New York: Silver Burdett Company, 1956.

Pitts, Lilla Belle, et al. The Kindergarten Book, enlarged edition. ("Our Singing World.") Boston: Ginn and Company, 1959.

_____. The First Grade Book, enlarged edition. ("Our Singing World.") Boston: Ginn and Company, 1959.

_____. Singing on Our Way, enlarged edition. ("Our Singing World.") Boston: Ginn and Company, 1959.

Sur, William Raymond, et al. "This Is Music," Books 1 and 2. Boston: Allyn and Bacon, Inc., 1962.

Wilson, Harry R., et al. "Growing with Music," Books 1 and 2. Englewood Cliffs, N.J.: Prentice-Hall, Inc., 1963.

Wolfe, Irving W., et al. Music 'Round the Clock. ("Together We Sing.") Chicago: Follett Publishing Company, 1955.

—————. Music 'Round the Town. ("Together We Sing.") Chicago: Follett Publishing Company, 1955.

—————. Music Through the Year. ("Together We Sing.") Chicago: Follett Publishing Company, 1956.

Other Useful Books

Coleman, Satis N., and Thorn, Alice G. Another Singing Time. New York: John Day Company, 1937.

—————. Singing Time. New York: John Day Company, 1929.

Hoffelt, Robert O. How to Lead Informal Singing. Nashville: Abingdon Press, 1963.

Landeck, Beatrice. More Songs to Grow On. New York: William Sloane Associates, 1954.

—————. Songs to Grow On. New York: William Sloane Associates, 1950.

Miller, Mary and Zajan, Paula. Finger Play. New York: G. Schirmer, Inc., 1955.

Seeger, Ruth C. American Folk Songs for Children. Garden City, N.Y.: Doubleday and Company, Inc., 1948.

Recordings

The companies listed below all have catalogs of children's material available. Some are more detailed than others. Listening to the recording or using it with children is still the only way to find out which recordings will be successful with your particular group. It is often necessary to experiment with many records before finding the right music for your group.

The three companies listed directly below handle children's records of all companies. They give quick mail service and frequently list records not available elsewhere, such as 78 rpm singles:

Children's Music Center, 2858 West Pico Boulevard, Los Angeles, Calif.
Children's Reading Service, 1078 St. John's Place, Brooklyn, N. Y.
Educational Record Sales, 153 Chambers Street, New York, N. Y.

The educational division of each of the following companies has a classified catalog available:
Capitol Records, 1750 North Vine Street, Hollywood, California 90028
Columbia Records, Inc., 799 Seventh Avenue, New York, N. Y.
Decca Records, 619 West 57th Street, New York, N. Y.
RCA Victor Records, 155 East 24th Street, New York, N. Y.

In addition, the following have helpful material:
Bowmar Records, 10515 Burbank Boulevard, North Hollywood, Calif. Selections designed for

children with special needs, also play-party games, rhythms, and children's literature.

Children's Record Guild and Young People's Records, Greystone Corporation, 100 Sixth Avenue, New York, N. Y. Many useful activity records; creative expression.

Folkraft, 1159 Broad Street, Newark, N. J. Dance syllabus for the elementary school available; folk dances and singing games; directions on every record cover.

Folkways Records and Service Corporation, 121 West 47th Street, New York, N. Y. Several of the selections in this book are available on "Learning as We Play" and "More Learning as We Play." This company specializes in folk music of the world and has an exceptional collection of Americana which may be adapted for use with children.

Little Golden Records, 1230 Sixth Avenue, New York, N. Y. Many excellent and economical songs and other materials; however, as these recordings are available for a limited time from the date of release, it is advisable to purchase extra copies as soon as possible when you discover an especially successful one.

Instruments

Rhythm instruments are available from educational supply houses and from many music stores. The companies listed here manufacture instruments and distribute throughout the country. Each has a catalog available:

Harmolin, Inc., P. O. Box 244, La Jolla, Calif. .... resonator bells

B. F. Kitching and Company, Inc., Brookfield, Ill. .... melody bells, bell blocks, ... triangles

Peripole Products, Inc., 51-17 Rockaway Beach .... melody, rhythm, and harmony Boulevard, Far Rockaway, Long Island, N. Y. .... instruments, step-bells

Oscar Schmidt International, Inc., 19 Ferry Street, Jersey City, N. J. .... autoharps

INDEX OF SONGS AND MUSIC